Marcus Jacob Goldman and L.

What to Do After You Say "I Do"

FROM THE PROPOSAL THROUGH

THE FIRST YEAR OF MARRIAGE:

A COUPLE'S GUIDE TO BUILDING

A HEALTHY FOUNDATION

PRIMA PUBLISHING

Prima Publishing and colophon are registered trademarks of Prima Communications, Inc.

Library of Congress Cataloging-in-Publication Data

Goldman, Marcus Jacob.
    What to do after you say "I do" : from the proposal through the first year of marriage : a couple's guide to building a healthy foundation / Marcus Jacob Goldman and Lori J. Goldman.
      p.   cm.
    Includes index.
    ISBN 0-7615-1159-8
    1. Marriage. 2. Communication in marriage. I. Goldman, Lori J. II. Title.
HQ734.G59 1997
646.7'8—dc21   97-35045
                                                                CIP

98 99 00 01 AA 10 9 8 7 6 5 4 3 2 1

Printed in the United States of America

How to Order
Single copies may be ordered from Prima Publishing, P.O. Box 1260BK, Rocklin, CA 95677; telephone (916) 632-4400. Quantity discounts are also available. On your letterhead, include information concerning the intended use of the books and the number of books you wish to purchase.

Visit us online at http://www.primapublishing.com

To my brother Hal and sister Jennifer, with love, affection, and gratitude.
— MJG

To my parents, Ben and Elaine, who gave me my roots.
To my three precious boys—Alex, Zachary, and Jacob—who give me
joy every day and who make me look toward tomorrow.
To my husband, who has made my life complete.
— LJG

About the Authors

MARCUS JACOB GOLDMAN, M.D., trained in general psychiatry at Harvard Medical School, where he also completed the Gaughan Fellowship in forensic psychiatry. Dr. Goldman is a member of the Program in Psychiatry and Law at Harvard and is board certified in general, forensic, and geriatric psychiatry. He has taught psychiatry and behavioral health at Harvard, has published numerous articles on a wide variety of mental-health issues, and is also the cofounder of an organization dedicated to helping psychiatrists pass their board examinations. His other books include *The Joy of Fatherhood: The First Twelve Months* (Prima) and *Kleptomania: The Compulsion to Steal—What Can Be Done?* (New Horizon). Dr. Goldman is medical director of New England Geriatrics.

LORI J. GOLDMAN, R.N., graduated from the Newhouse School of Public Communications at Syracuse University. She is also a registered nurse and has practiced in emergency room, intensive care, and pediatric facilities. She is currently the mother of three busy boys and lives in Massachusetts. This is the first book she has co-authored.

Contents

Acknowledgments

As usual, I've come to rely on a variety of important people for practical advice and spiritual help. Without them, bits and pieces of this book might very well still be sitting inside my computer. To these people, I'm eternally grateful:

To my children, for their unwavering enthusiasm and love of life; to my wife, Lori, for her love, support, and guidance, and for constructively dealing with my dirty jokes; to my agent, Margaret Russell, for her strength and inspiration; to my brother Hal and sister Jennifer for their advice, love, and collective senses of humor; to my grandmother Sarah, for her encouragement and wisdom; and to my parents for their support, perseverance, and strength.

I'd also like to thank Dave Wasserman, C.P.A., the number cruncher; Ellen Glickman-Simon for her time and help with some of the legal issues presented in this book; Gregg Sulkin for his assistance in educating me all over again; Ed Carp, for his tips, advice, and friendship; Bill Land for his motivational discussions and great ideas; and Tom Gutheil for his continued support and encouragement.

I feel especially lucky to be working again with the great people at Prima, Ben Dominitz, Jamie Miller, and Michelle McCormack. I appreciate their confidence in me.

Finally, writing a book takes time and support. I'd like to thank Steve Marcus and everyone else at New England Geriatrics for giving me both. Thanks for making it easy for me and making me feel a part of something very special.

— MJG

I'd like to thank the many people who offered their stories—some were very personal—for this book. I also owe a debt of gratitude to the following people for their support, friendship, and encouragement: Alissa Wein, Debra Sherman-Shrier, Audrey Bressler, Mary-Ann Guild, and Nancy Dicks.

—LJG

Introduction

Welcome to the first year of marriage. What an exciting time! The institution of marriage—a dream-come-true for many, a thrilling stage in life for others—is a remarkable, time-tested tradition. Full of meaning, mutual commitment, love, and romance, there's nothing quite like it. Whether you're inching toward matrimony, standing at its threshold, or have already taken the plunge, many new and exciting experiences await you. Even if you're still exploring your options, or just starting to make wedding plans, this book will provide you with critically useful information. *What to Do After You Say "I Do"* will also pose some questions along the way. Why? Because when two people get together, amazing—and sometimes confusing—things can happen. Like any other new endeavor that requires emotional investment, getting married (and, for that matter, staying married) takes practice, experience, and perseverance.

Exploring the unique new feelings and experiences associated with marriage is well worth your time. Most ideas about marriage (good, bad, or both) come from observing our parents' relationships. For some, the resulting wedding fantasy encompasses a carefree jaunt—a happy couple skipping effortlessly down the aisle looking forward to a lifetime of fulfillment with each other. For others, marriage conjures up images of being drugged and forced down the aisle by demonic cupids, headed toward a life of certain torture and endless misery. Complicated stuff.

For most of us though, the fantasy lands somewhere between sheer terror and idealized harmony. Looking back at my own case, despite being engaged to a wonderful woman, my vision included a little of both misery and delight. Would it last or would we fail? Paradoxically, I remember feeling overjoyed but petrified. How could I have had such differing feelings all at once? Two reasons: Nothing that matters is ever just a walk in the park *and* you can't be experienced or certain about something you've never done before. Somewhere in the back of my pre-wedding mind, I knew that I'd have a lot of work to do to keep this thing moving forward.

Marriage is *work*? Sometimes. The truth is that while most people become acutely anxious if their checkbooks don't balance, for example, they don't bother to invest enough time making sure their marriages are balanced. Who wants to fall behind on something as important as preparing to spend the rest of your life with another person? Do you feel apprehensive or ambivalent about your decision to marry? You're not alone. When I started writing this book, I recalled a wonderful story I had heard through my work as a consultant in geriatric psychiatry. A young therapist who had recently been married was interviewing a very elderly patient. Seeking the wisdom of an obviously experienced person, the therapist asked the patient how her marriage had been, to which the elderly woman replied after serious thought, "Well, the first forty years were tough, but the last twenty were a breeze."

Marriage often entails hard work, understanding, misunderstanding, and conflict. Before my wedding I knew that the toughest part of being married would be accepting the uncertainty that always accompanies any undertaking that really matters. The good news? There's plenty! You'll be spending your life with the person of your choice— someone you respect, cherish, and admire. The two of you will have wonderful times together, sharing intimacy, traveling, spending time just talking, nurturing the relationship, and loving each other. What a great way to go through life's journey!

Marriage has always conjured up lots of questions. How could it not? Are there ways to start off on the right track? What sort of marriages will survive, thrive, and flourish, and which will falter, fail, and end in disaster? As my own wedding approached, and even though I'd spent thousands of hours with my wife-to-be, as a man I still had lots of questions: How can I possibly be part of a permanent couple when I'm so used to being independent? What if I meet someone I like better? Will we become a divorce statistic? Can we stay friends? Do I really love this person? What's the difference between love and lust? Will I have free time for myself, or do we have to spend every moment together? And so on.

I wondered if men and women shared the same concerns. Well, as it turned out, my wife-to-be had questions too. Some of her questions were the same as mine, but others took on a decidedly less selfish tone: Am I getting married for the right reasons? Will he be a good husband? What kind of father will he be? What sort of wife will I be to him?

That's why it's so important to look closely at the first year of marriage. It's good to start off right. In my other book *The Joy of Fatherhood*, I emphasized the importance of parents working together during the baby's first year to ensure an environment rich in love and cooperation for the future. Likewise, you will carry much of what happens during the first year of marriage—the way you treat one another, show your love, resolve conflict, and work together to better yourselves—into the rest of your lives. Imagine your first year of marriage as a template upon which you will base the experiences of a lifetime together. This year clearly has enormous implications for your fledgling family. In addition to your own happiness as a couple, a healthy marriage drastically increases the chances of raising emotionally well-adjusted children.

Are the questions ever resolved completely or is marriage a work-in-progress? Interestingly enough, ten years and three kids after my wedding, a few of my initial concerns still reappear with a frequency that surprises me, although it shouldn't. I always seem to be asking questions and searching for answers. We often assume marriage should be a partnership of steadfast permanence, but it's also an institution that seems to be in dynamic flux—always changing, moving, and sloshing around. Dealing with the uncertainty is the tough part.

Recognizing, understanding, and accepting these many diverse feelings is central to a happy life together.

Before I got married, I searched for a resource to help me deal with my questions, address my momentary lapses into uncertainty, and accompany me through the memorable wonders of the first year with my new wife. *What to Do After You Say "I Do"* seeks to provide you with answers to complicated but common concerns and questions. While the real goal of *What to Do After You Say "I Do"* is to highlight the unparalleled joys of marriage, this book will also help the two of you stay on track by encouraging communication, mutual respect, love, and admiration.

Who Wrote This Book?

As I frequently do in life, in writing this book I asked my wife, Lori J. Goldman, for some help. Although it seems like just yesterday that my proud parents were nudging me down the aisle, ten years later, my wife and I are still together, sorting through the good and bad times together, as the best teams do. In writing a book like *What to Do After You Say "I Do"* I understood the importance of presenting different perspectives on the subjects we will explore. There are always at least two sides to everything. Marriage is no exception. What better way to explore these perspectives than to hear from husband *and* wife? This book is a joint effort, but for clarity and simplicity most of it is written in the first person.

What's in This Book?

What to Do After You Say "I Do" is designed to help both of you learn to grow together during your first year of marriage. We'll spend a lot of time highlighting the wonders of your loving relationship with each other, but we'll also look at other equally important issues. Some books on marriage avoid dealing directly and bluntly with both the good and the tough parts of marriage. *What to Do After You Say "I Do"* won't shy away from tough-to-talk-about issues. While we'll cover the basics—to wed or not to wed, the honeymoon, growing together—we'll also look at potentially divisive issues.

How Is This Book Organized?

What to Do After You Say "I Do" consists of twelve chapters. With the exception of the first chapter, which deals with the issue of whether or not to get married, each chapter will explore the various phases of your first year together. For ease of reading and consistency, the chapters are organized similarly and may contain some or all of the following sections:

WHAT'S NEW WITH THE TWO OF YOU?

This section contains important information about what may be happening at a specific stage in the relationship.

WHAT ARE YOU FEELING OR THINKING?

While most people tend to keep their most personal thoughts or feelings to themselves—both positive and negative—this section brings these feelings out into the open.

OVERCOMING YOUR NEW OBSTACLES

No relationship is without a major obstacle every now and then. This section endeavors to locate and smooth out the rocky roads.

IT JUST KEEPS GETTING BETTER

Ideally, your marriage will be joyous and mutually beneficial. In this section, we'll explore what it is that makes for a great marriage.

BEING THERE FOR EACH OTHER

How can you stay involved with your partner? Why is it essential? What steps can you take to remain close to one another? How can you provide for your husband or wife by providing for yourself? This section will help you "be there" for each other—both physically and emotionally. Dealing with difficult-to-manage feelings, we'll explore ways in which you can use your knowledge and hard work to maintain a healthy relationship with each other.

FOCUS

These sections contain objective, practical information, helpful how-to instructions, and crucial advice on a variety of relevant concerns.

YOUR LIFE TOGETHER

In this section, we'll summarize important issues raised or discussed in the chapter and review what's next, with an emphasis on growing and learning together as a couple.

Also included throughout the book are helpful tips, definitions, Questions and Answers Sections and updates covering a variety of issues. Couples' real-life experiences and thoughts are used to emphasize key issues and make tough subjects a little easier to face.

The Importance of Language

Language can often, without our knowledge, wreak havoc on people's sensibilities. In an attempt to be reasonable, and to avoid as much controversy as possible, I've randomly altered gender throughout the book, using, for example, "husband" or "wife," "him" or "her," "boyfriend" or "girlfriend," rather than constantly employing the neutral and impersonal "spouse."

Final Words

In addition to being fun, marriage is, in essence, a mutual investment— by far the most important you'll ever make. There's a lot to gain and a lot to lose. Your marriage will form the basis of family life, not only for you, but for many generations to come. Along with marriage's many pleasures come sacrifice, hard work, and compromise. The ways in which you live your lives together during the first year shape your future together. You can make no more valuable an investment than to honor each other with patience and meaningful communication. It's our sincere hope that *What to Do After You Say "I Do"* will not only help you learn these valuable skills, but will also accompany you on your first-year adventures and help prepare you for your life together.

· 1 ·

Should We or Shouldn't We?

CONTEMPLATING THE BIG STEP

1

Should we or shouldn't we? That's the question! For many couples, based on their mutual love and positive experiences together, the decision to marry is an easy one:

"Right from the very start of our courtship, we both decided that our relationship should inevitably end in either marriage or just end. As it turned out, neither of us gave marriage a second, nervous thought. We just did it."

For other couples, the decision is a bit more involved. Thinking about getting married is not nearly as straightforward as buying a new car, getting a job, or buying more memory for your computer. In fact, just thinking about marriage can be quite challenging. If you find yourselves in this situation, try your best to see the decision-making process as a unique and exciting time in your lives. After all, while making important decisions can sometimes feel lonely and stressful, the two of you have each other to talk with and love while you're deciding.

Sometimes, thinking about a commitment as major as marriage can be overwhelming. Our thoughts can tip-toe up behind us, pat us lightly on the shoulder, and gently nudge us forward toward a decision. Other times, our thoughts stomp up and stab us forcefully in the back.

> Marriage is not a race. Think about getting married slowly, over time—not all at once.

There's nothing worse than feeling ambushed by our own thoughts. But for many of us, thinking about marriage has *always* been that way—black or white, do or don't. The truth? There's room for a mixture of feelings. Idealized images of marriage are nice, but the reality is that thinking about getting married makes for interesting, sometimes confusing, and often provocative discussion:

"Before I knew it, I was faced with the single most important decision of my life. All my previous seemingly crucial decisions—what color car to buy; what school to go to; how to conduct myself in public; pepperoni, mushroom, or cheese—all pale in comparison. Nothing could have prepared me for this moment."

Whether the two of you are thinking about marriage, or thinking about thinking about marriage, one thing is certain: No single decision will have as far reaching a result. Regardless of your current relationship with each other, nothing as meaningful as marriage could or should be simple to decide:

"Well, to be honest, first, neither of us were thinking about marriage. Then, I was thinking about it, but she wasn't. Then, when I had decided not to think about it, she wanted to give it some thought. Then, neither of us wanted to think about it. Frankly, I didn't really understand what the heck was going on. Sometimes I think it's tough to come together on the issue."

Don't worry, the ambivalence is reversible! It had better be, or no one would ever get married. How many people have mixed feelings? At some point along the road to marriage, just about everyone. In fact, mixed feelings are ubiquitous and don't at all negate love:

"My then-boyfriend was so opposed to the very concept of getting married—to anyone, let alone me—that I thought we were headed for certain doom. He told me he'd rather drink motor oil than get married. Now, he's my husband. I guess he got over it."

Is it reasonable to anticipate a rough or complicated decision-making process? For some of us, the nature of the deliberations can be complex—two different people, dozens of different perspectives. Despite your differences or similarities, getting married—even entering into a discussion about marriage—usually takes a great deal of careful thought and planning.

> Don't view ambivalence as a liability. Unclear feelings will take you to new heights of uncertainty and bewilderment. This may make for some very interesting drama, which is most often followed by creative solutions.

What are you feeling? Would it help to know what others are thinking and feeling? What are some common thoughts among people faced with this momentous decision? What influences how you're making the decision? What are some of the obstacles to overcome? Do you need to resolve all of them, or can your thoughts be a work-in-progress? Are there important risks and benefits to be considered? How can you ever really be certain?

> 🌀 Take some time alone—maybe a weekend away from each other—to thoroughly reflect on your feelings about getting married. Use the time to sort out what you feel certain about and what causes ambivalence or anxiety.

While there are no easy or definitive answers, sometimes just identifying your varied feelings can lessen the anxiety. Being aware of your certainties *and* uncertainties can really lighten the emotional load. You may be surprised to discover that others—perhaps even your boyfriend or girlfriend—share some of your feelings. In this chapter, we'll take a look at some important thoughts, feelings, and issues that often emerge as you make your way through the wonderfully worthwhile decision-making process.

What's New with the Two of You?

What's new? Just about everything. Just how tough can it be? Even pondering your options together can become a formidable task—especially if you don't see eye-to-eye. How fun can it be? Well, depending on what the two of you decide to do, your decision may well lead to a lifetime of excitement and love. Whether you've lived together or not, for many couples, the idea of becoming a fiancé conjures up a variety of feelings—some positive and some negative. Not surprisingly, both men and women often have similar feelings, thoughts, and concerns, but often keep the issues to themselves. Let's take a look.

YOU MAY BE THINKING ABOUT . . .

Lack of Experience in Long-Term Relationships Not uncommonly, some couples have had relatively little experience staying with one person for any great length of time. This fact alone can lead to anxiety:

> *"The longest relationship I ever had with a man was about eight months. The longest relationship my boyfriend ever had before me was about eight minutes. Now, we're faced with the proposition of marriage—that's theoretically and hopefully for life. I'm afraid we just don't have the kind of relationship experience necessary for this new 'job'."*

Although we'll look more closely at this issue later on, have no fear. There's no time requirement or mandatory on-the-job training for marriage. Marriage, as we'll see, is a shared experienced made better with the passage of time, discussion, and patience.

Your Feelings of Love While you may have your own particular set of questions, thoughts, or concerns, it's certainly common and desirable to have feelings of unwavering love and admiration for your significant other. For many couples, the decision-making process is overshadowed by a desire to just be together:

> *"I know that the decision to get married can be tough, but we're in love, and I'm sure that everything else will fall into place."*

Past Relationships Becoming engaged means that you've given up your freedom to physically relive past romantic relationships. Despite this, it's very clear that memories of old flames may reappear, or may even intensify:

"We got engaged last week. Since then, I've been thinking about my old girlfriend constantly. It's kind of weird. We haven't seen each other in years, yet I can't get her out of my mind. I guess I'm giving her one long last emotional look. It's almost like shaking the tree before I settle in."

Sometimes, these memories can be difficult for the other partner to listen to. This can lead to a less-than-desirable result:

"After we got engaged, my fiancée started talking about her old boyfriend. It's driving me crazy. She never really talked about him before. But now I find myself insanely jealous. If she doesn't stop soon, I'm going to call him up and ask him what his secret was."

Provided that such thoughts or fantasies don't lead to actions, they are usually nothing more than that—a trip down old, familiar territory; one last visit before the commitment is final. Although most of us will always remember the formative experiences and relationships that helped shape the way we approach our current relationship, in most cases these thoughts will eventually fade.

Try to keep jealousy in perspective. Remember, there were reasons the old relationships didn't last.

Spending the Rest of Your Life with One Person What a concept! Many of us can't imagine living with one person forever:

"When my girlfriend told me that she wasn't going to wait around forever, I thought she was waiting for a bus or something. It didn't

dawn on me that she wanted to live with me forever. Nice denial, I guess."

"I can barely live with myself. When my girlfriend told me she wanted to get married, I was at once struck with a deep sense of nausea and despair I simply did not understand."

How Relieved You Are to Have Found the "Perfect" Mate

Many couples feel relieved that they've found someone to spend the rest of their lives with, and seem less concerned with the engagement process:

"After spending all those years dating creeps and misfits who have nothing in common with me, I was so happy to have finally found a creep and misfit with similar values to mine. But seriously, now that I have found someone, I couldn't care less about the anxiety associated with engagement and marriage. Let the wedding bells ring!"

Your Role as Husband or Wife

It's perfectly natural to feel anxious about your ability to be a good husband or wife:

"I've never been a husband before. What do I do? Is there some book I should read?"

Fearful they'll repeat their parents' mistakes, some people choose not to marry, or to delay the inevitable for as long as possible:

"I certainly shouldn't use what I learned watching my parents in their so-called relationship. All they did was beat up emotionally on each other. It was terrible. My boyfriend tries to reassure me, but I'm still petrified."

Whether Your Mate Will Be a Good Marriage Partner

You may also be concerned about your boyfriend or girlfriend's ability to fulfill the role of husband or wife:

"My boyfriend's father is a terrible gambler. We don't gamble much, but I'm worried that once the pressures of married life begin, he might take it up."

⊗ Sometimes seeking counsel or advice from a trusted member of the clergy can help reduce your anxiety. This person may be able to help you talk about issues you are worried about but can't share with your potential spouse.

Whether Your Spouse Will Be a Good Parent Clearly an important consideration, your significant other's ability to cope constructively with the stress of raising kids should be considered. Like anything else in life, nothing is ever certain:

"How am I supposed to tell if my boyfriend will be good with kids? He's never really been around them."

In Chapter 11, we'll take a closer look at parenthood issues.

Whether You'll Retain Your Independence Many people are concerned that their autonomy and sense of individuality will be stripped away once they're married. Some concerns are subtler than others:

"Will I be like a dog on a leash?"

"I'm used to getting up when I want, going to bed when I want, eating when I want. What's it going to be like for me to have to share everything with another person? How is this going to work out?"

Usually, the benefits of living with the person you love make up for any concerns you might have about issues of time and space. In Chapter 6 we'll take a closer look at these often divisive issues.

> Although it's tempting, try not to hold the sins of the fathers (or mothers) against the sons (or daughters). Unless your mate is engaging in obviously destructive behavior, consider your significant other to have a set of values and behaviors separate from his or her parents' bad habits.

Whether You Can Stay Faithful Paralyzed by a fear of infidelity, some people continue to delay marriage:

"I'm no Don Juan—I'm actually more like a 'Ron' Juan—but I dated a lot in college. I'm fearful that I won't be able to stay true to my potential wife-to-be. I don't want to stray, but I'm afraid I might. I don't want to become a statistic. I think that's why I just can't commit to engagement at this point. I'll just wait a bit longer."

Likewise, a sometimes rational, sometimes irrational inability to trust one's significant other can be a problem:

"I know it sounds horrible, but I've had such terrible times with men in the past. My boyfriend is dying to get married (to me, I think), but I just don't think I can trust him enough to marry him. What if he cheats on me?"

As we'll see later on, for one reason or another, about 50 percent of all marriages end in divorce—affairs and other indiscretions being responsible for some failures. The statistics seem overwhelming, but we'll look at some simple ways you can successfully defy the odds.

Whether You're Marrying for the Right Reasons As we'll see, the reasons for getting married are about as varied as the reasons not to take the plunge.

QUESTIONS AND ANSWERS

Why Do People Get Married?

Part of "should we or shouldn't we?" really has a lot to do with making decisions together—something you'll want to do for the rest of your lives if you decide to wed. After a lot of soul searching, the two of you may decide that marriage is not for you. As long as your decisions are informed and the result of serious thought and not impulse, you really can't go wrong. Clearly, the ways in which you arrive at your decision are as important as the decisions themselves.

As you chart the course of your life together, and although you'll likely always have many concerns and questions, it's important not to lose sight of your ability to grow and learn together. Going through the good and bad times as a team and talking about your experiences and feelings together is crucial.

We've already looked at some common concerns and feelings, but does everyone have the same ideas about marriage? What are the reasons for getting married? What contributes to people's ideas about whether or not to wed? In this question-and-answer section, we'll take a look at different perspectives on this not-so-clear issue.

Q: I'm thinking about proposing to my girlfriend, although I'm a little confused. I think I love her. I mean, I get very excited sexually when we're together. Isn't this a good sign?

A: Sure. Love, and being in love, should definitely form the basis upon which everything else in your lives together is built. There's a big difference between love and lust, however. The issue of love must transcend the objective concepts of physical attraction and sex.

Q: I'm having some trouble with the notion of marrying my boyfriend. One of the things I've noticed is that he loves being with me all the time, while I tend to need a bit of space now and then. I know that being together is important—and I do love being with him—but not all the time. Are our styles of interacting with each other consistent with those of two people who should get married?

A: Enjoying your time together is an important part of dating, engagement, and marriage. It would not make sense if you did not want to be together. You can find a middle ground, however. In fact, as you both grow together, there will invariably be times when you don't see eye-to-eye. Of course, part of working together as a team also means resolving conflicts related to your own sense of individuality. Later in this book we'll discuss important "time and space" issues.

Q: This is going to sound very odd, but my personality type is such that I feel almost lost unless I'm in a long-term relationship. I'm like a golden retriever—I need lots of attention. I tend to rely on my significant others for a variety of things that are important to me. I'm also fearful of spending the rest of my life alone. I hate boredom and isolation and want to feel financially secure. I've been dating a man now for over two years and I want to marry him. Is the fulfillment of my dependency needs a good enough reason to get married?

A: Taken on its own, probably not. But people get married for all kinds of reasons—including the fulfillment of a variety of emotional and practical needs. Remember, everybody has his or her own unique style. It seems very unlikely that the only thing you find attractive about your boyfriend is the fact that he provides for you in certain ways. It's possible—even desirable—to marry for many reasons, one of which might include a reason that on its own doesn't seem sufficient.

Q: *Sometimes I worry that I'm entering into marriage for ill-conceived reasons. For example, it simply seems convenient for me to get married now. Also, there's a part of me that feels as though I need to be in control of the relationship—almost controlling the other person. Should I avoid marriage?*

A: Some people believe in running towards adversity, while others tend to shy away from it. If you're sophisticated enough to recognize these personal characteristics and question how they affect you, you're clearly better off than those who would deny them. We'll look more closely at this important issue later.

Q: *For me, marriage is the ultimate, logical step towards personal fulfillment as a woman. I want to have kids and raise a family. It seems like my boyfriend and I have many shared values and similar religious convictions and we both like the feeling of personal responsibility and commitment. I know diversity has its advantages. Is there anything wrong though with being too similar?*

A: No.

Q: *I'm kind of like a Reagan Republican while my fiancée is sort of like a McGovern Democrat. Is there any hope for us?*

A: Politics makes strange bedfellows and so, too, I guess, does marriage. Diversity will make for some interesting discussions, but as long as you share common values and are open and honest about your differences, you really can't go wrong.

Q: I've been dating the same woman now for two years. We have a great time and she wants to get married. My parents are pushing me toward marriage. They want grandchildren. I told them they could rent some. I don't want to not get married in the service of rebelling against my parents, but I can't sort it all out. What should I do?

A: Some people get married because they feel it will bring their parents happiness and/or because it is easier to submit to the pressures—either unspoken and subtle or frank and obvious—than continue to "rebel." But getting married simply because your family wants you to is ill-advised. But again, most people wed for a variety of reasons. Pleasing one's parents, as long as you're getting married also to please yourself and your wife-to-be, is perfectly acceptable.

Q: I'm getting married because I'm pregnant. What do you think of that?

A: Depending on one's personal convictions and beliefs, this may clearly make sense. Ideally, you and your husband-to-be have other reasons for marrying as well.

Q: One of the reasons I'm getting married—I know this sounds infantile—is because I'm afraid of getting a sexually transmitted disease. I don't have a lot of sexual experience—actually, I have none. But I figure if we both stay true to each other, sexually transmitted diseases are one fewer thing to worry about.

A: Nothing wrong with that, provided of course that your other reasons for getting married are sound.

FOCUS

Why Not Just Live Together?

Living together has been the subject of movies and television shows for years. In the free-love 1960s, you were considered strange if you didn't live together. You may be living together right now. For several decades—ever since the '60s, when living together became a culturally acceptable substitute for marriage—people have actively debated the issue:

"I would never live with my boyfriend. Once he's got the product, why would he ever propose to me? There's no way I'll live with him until I get a ring and a commitment."

For some couples, living together before marriage seems like a sort of extended trial period—a time when the "product" (either partner) can be returned for a full cash refund, so to speak. For others, living together can become a permanent arrangement that never leads to marriage. What are some of the common issues and feelings associated with living together? One or both members of a couple may feel:

Being There for Each Other

We've seen how couples feel about marriage and looked at the reasons people list for tying the knot. What's the best way, given all this information, to make that everlasting, all-important decision? If you're like a lot of people, somewhere in the back of your mind you're harboring a healthy dose of ambivalence about the whole process. Unfortunately, there aren't any road maps or easy answers. But all is not lost!

- Rebellious: *"I don't get it. What's the big deal? My parents are all bent out of shape and have all but disowned me. I sort of like inflaming them."*

- A Sense of Convenience: *"We lived together for a long time before we got married. I had to push my boyfriend to get married. Since he had everything he wanted any time— namely me—he had no incentive to get married. I'll bet if I had refused to live with him, he would have married me much sooner."*

- Frightened of Commitment: *"Marriage is such a final event. It's legally binding and enmeshing. Who needs it? My girlfriend and I talk about it all the time. I'm just not ready for marriage. If we're just living together, one of us, or both, can always just walk out—no strings attached."*

- Fearful of Altering the Status Quo: *"My significant other and I have been living together for years. We have a son. Nobody really knows that we're not married. It seems like such a pain in the neck. I don't want to ruin what we have. What does it matter anyway?"*

(continued on next page)

When you get ready to make your way through the thick underbrush of the decision-making process, grab your machete and chop through the questions on the Focus section "Thirteen Questions to Ask Yourselves and Each Other" (page 20). They will bring together ideas and, most likely, points of agreement and disagreement about a variety of issues. Think carefully about each question and share your thoughts with your boyfriend. Think out loud with him.

Most of the time, these questions will lead to discussions about a variety of important topics, which can help the two of you decide if

(Focus—continued)

- Morally Opposed: *"Marriage never went well for my parents— or their parents. Why repeat the mistakes of the past?"*
- Obligated to "Try Out" the Arrangement Before Marriage: *"What do I do if I marry her and then find someone I like better? Living with her first seems like a good way to make sure that doesn't happen."*
- Entitled: *"Why should I buy the product without first having tried it out?"*
- Perfectly Content: *"We never ask ourselves why we're taking this course of action. We love being with each other and are completely satisfied with this arrangement."*
- Cornered: *"I know he'll never marry me. He can't commit. He's been a bachelor for too long. Living together is the only way I can be with him."*

Despite the many factors involved with living together, permanently, or as a trial period before marriage, one thing is clear: Marriage seems to afford couples a way to commit to each other in a way that those who live together don't necessarily have to consider. Whether or not you decide to "cohabitate" is a personal decision. Statistically, those who live together before they are married tend not to have as successful marriages as those who don't live together before marriage. Go figure.

marriage is the right course. Remember, the way you spend your first year of marriage—the way you treat one another, resolve problems constructively, and so on—will form the foundation on which you'll build the rest of your lives together. Establishing good communication skills early—long before the wedding bells ring—is a crucial part of a successful marriage.

These questions are meant to be pondered over time. Again, there aren't any right or wrong answers, and agreement on points certainly won't guarantee a peaceful marriage. Go slowly, think together, and have fun!

It Just Keeps Getting Better

Congratulations! If you're reading this section, and haven't thrown the book out after having found you have nothing in common with the person you've been involved with for four years, then things must be going well. For some couples, the engagement process seems effortless:

"It was magical. He told me to pack a bag—I thought he was kicking me out. Then we flew to our favorite city. He took me to an expensive restaurant and asked me. It was a complete surprise, but really so easy."

"My girlfriend and I spent a quiet evening alone at my place. The music was on and I had just cooked a great meal for her. Then I sat down beside her and gave her the ring. It was great."

Remember, questions and concerns about marriage have no right or wrong answers. Dialogue—with yourself and with your boyfriend or girlfriend—is the key. It's not a test. You don't need a #2 pencil.

FOCUS

Thirteen Questions to Ask Yourselves and Each Other

1. Why should we get married?
2. Why shouldn't we get married?
3. Will we be able to rejoice in our differences, or will we use them against each other?
4. Do we want to have children?
5. Given our differences and similarities (personality types, values, life philosophies), how will we work to learn and grow together?
6. Given our differences and similarities, how will we work together to raise a family?

For others, the moment of engagement comes after years of debate and conflict:

"My feeling was, 'It's about time.' The way he proposed was nothing special since we had been arguing about marriage right up until he finally asked me."

However the proposal happens, one thing is certain: The period around engagement and right up to the wedding can be a very exciting time, but it can also simultaneously be a time of some anxiety.

YOU MAY BE FEELING . . .

Thrilled Despite any other feeling that might emerge, most couples experience a rush of excitement and delight. Whether the engagement was a surprise, spontaneous, or well planned, the thrill of this special

7. What is your philosophy regarding money and financially related issues?

8. Do we share some common family-oriented goals, and if not, will we be able to negotiate the differences constructively?

9. After we are married, can we still spend time with others or on our own (clubs, friends, individual hobbies, etc.)?

10. Can we openly discuss concrete, practical matters constructively (household chores, financial issues, etc.)?

11. Will we be able to resolve our differences constructively?

12. What do you like most about me?

13. What worries you the most about me?

time is truly unparalleled. For some, the excitement starts with the day of engagement:

> *"The night we got engaged, we were so excited that we ran up a $200 phone bill. I called people I hadn't spoken to in years. It was just so special a time."*

> *"For us, getting engaged was just one stop along the route to marriage. It just kept getting better and better as the wedding approached."*

All in all, it really doesn't matter how or where the proposal occurs. What matters is your shared ideas about your lives together and the future:

> *"The engagement was great, sure, but what was really thrilling was the entire concept of us sharing our lives together in a far more definitive way."*

Relieved For some couples, the hours leading up to engagement have turned into days, which have turned into weeks, months, and years:

"We had talked about it briefly . . . for about six years. His proposal was no great surprise, but when it did happen, I was incredibly relieved."

Couples feel relieved for other reasons too:

"I felt like this burden had been lifted off my shoulders. I never thought I'd get married, and when she said 'yes,' I felt like my whole life had changed just in that instant. I guess it was a self-esteem thing."

> If possible, make the proposal special—not necessarily expensive. It helps to start paving the road with nice memories to reflect upon later.

Incredibly Romantic It's what you've been waiting for! Enjoy it. See the Focus section "Romance Update" (page 23), for some ideas to make it even better.

Stressed Out Is there room for stress? Engagement means that other things will necessarily follow—a greater responsibility toward each other, planning for the wedding, and eventual family duties, to name a few. For some, the excitement is tempered by both real and perceived stress:

"The engagement went fine and everything. Then one day, it just sort of hit me. What was I doing? I had so much to do. I had to be a fiancée, work, plan the wedding, find money, marry the guy, be a wife, keep working, find money, buy a house, have kids, grow old, retire, and die. Maybe I'm biting off more than I can chew."

FOCUS

Romance Update

Keep track of your romantic "firsts " with a special calendar or journal. Do the following:

- Make the date of your engagement a special day from that point on. Celebrate your one-month engagement "anniversary" by sharing a special intimate dinner together.
- Tape record, or record on your calendar, the first time you refer to your boyfriend as "my fiancé" when in public—or the first time he refers to you that way. That way you'll always remember it.
- Document the first time the two of you shopped together as an engaged couple.
- Write down the first person the two of you called when you became engaged. Keep that phone bill.
- Tape record your first conversation together as an engaged couple. What are your future plans? How are you feeling? Who will you tell first?

"I immediately felt like back-pedaling the minute she said 'yes.' This is too much to deal with right now."

As we'll see, after the marriage proposal and acceptance, you're bound to have mixed feelings—one of the healthy hallmarks of the human experience.

Ambivalent So you thought it would be all fun and games? Like almost everything else in life, uncertainty is probably sneaking around in the back of your minds:

"For me, and I feel guilty about this, there was this awful sense of final-ity. I couldn't see my old girlfriends anymore. I was gently encouraged by my fiancée not to even think *about them anymore. I'd never be able to touch another woman. Thank goodness I still have my ability to think privately."*

"I was delighted to be engaged, but I have to admit that I also felt this weird sense of loss, even regret, at the same time. I can't explain it, but in a way it felt like a good friend had just moved away. I guess there are parts of my life and past I'll just have to give up. I'm a little apprehen-sive. I hope I'm getting married for the right reasons."

While uncertainty is not necessarily a bad thing, some, unfortu-nately, feel compelled to act out their ambivalence:

"I'm engaged, but that doesn't mean I can't still see other women. I mean, I'm not married yet. I still see my old girlfriend and once in a while we fool around. As long as we don't have intercourse, I'm not cheating, right?"

> ❖ While planning for the future is fine, some-times dealing with the here and now is more important.

Pride and a Sense of Triumph Not uncommonly, men and women express great satisfaction about being engaged for a variety of reasons, not the least of which are feelings often unrelated to love:

"I'm walking around with this rock on my finger. I admit it, I feel great. I love it when other women comment on it."

"She had lots of serious boyfriends before me. Now she's mine. I got the girl. What a happy ending!"

So how do you manage this mishmash of feelings? Well, for the most part, there's nothing wrong with *enjoying* your mixed feelings. Most of the time, mixed feelings lead to open, honest discussions and creative solutions to complex problems. Also, if you're discussing your concerns, it's a good sign that you're not negatively acting out your feelings.

> Use uncertainty to your advantage. Your ultimate goal should be to express your ambivalence or conflicting feelings not through action, but through dialogue. Practicing these skills now will help your marriage succeed.

In the best-case scenario, your engagement came at a time when the two of you have openly explored many of the tough questions together. New issues will always come up—uncertainty, anxiety, and pressures. If you've taken the time to let discussion, compromise, and patience help you resolve your conflicts and concerns, there's a good chance you can solve any future problems too. Remember, finding the right person is a dream-come-true. Congratulations!

Your Life Together

Phew! Who knew engagement could be so complicated? Keep in mind, though, that it's just one step in a long but fabulous process. Don't forget that you will repeat the ideals and styles you establish early on over and over. Your future family will be affected by the decisions the two of you make today. Do yourself a favor: Stick together and work through this thought-provoking and potentially confusing time. It will pay off. In the next chapter, we'll look at the variety of intense feelings associated with the big day: your wedding.

· 2 ·

Taking the Plunge

A TRIP DOWN THE AISLE

2

So far so good. Time to relax? Well, not exactly:

> "*Time to plan for the wedding? Wow! There's a lot to do!*"

Of course, you *have* been through a lot of the tough stuff already: He's popped the question, she's said "yes"—or something along those lines. Now what? Well, if you're like many couples, you've probably spent the better part of a year or more planning for the wedding—that *is* hard work. Is there still time to enjoy each other? The time between engagement and the wedding can actually provide both of you with a wonderfully unique opportunity:

> "*We had so much fun together the year prior to the wedding. After we got engaged, it was like the pressure was off. We were free to be ourselves. We traveled together, made plans, sat around and did nothing together. We pretended we were already married and talked a lot about how our lives together would change once we were finally married.*"

Of course, there's hard work ahead as well:

> "*We picked out plates. We picked out glasses—how many different types of cups can there be? We picked out silverware—I could fund my retirement*"

with three of these spoons. We picked out cases where the spoons will live so that when we never use them, they'll be safe. I've listened to more bands and DJs in the past two weeks than in my entire life. We've argued about seating arrangements and the fact that my uncle, who hates my aunt's brother, wants to be allowed to smoke his stinky cigars at the wedding. To tell you the truth, our lives have become so consumed by the wedding, if it weren't for our collective senses of humor, we'd be lost!"

Men sometimes fail to accompany their fiancées to department stores to pick out place settings or other important items. The items you bring into the house are really important statements that the two of you should make together. Try not to get into the routine of assuming that the woman should do the shopping.

Whether the wedding will be large, small, or in-between, the emotional energy expended in the preparing for these most important few hours is huge. As the day approaches, you may be thinking about any number of things. All in all, though, chances are pretty good that the wedding will go smoothly and that you'll both have the time of your life. How's it going? What are you feeling? In this chapter, we'll take a look at the complexities, anxieties, and pleasures of coming in for that long-awaited landing down the aisle.

What's New with the Two of You?

Planning your futures together can be great fun. Nothing, however, is fun all the time:

> *"Nowhere was it ever written that preparing for marriage would be so time consuming. I want this thing to go off without a hitch, but there are so many variables—many things beyond my control—that I'm worried it'll never happen."*

In fact, you've probably had to overcome many interesting and new obstacles. Here are a few of the dozens of things you two have had to do, plan, think about, or accomplish:

- *Proposing:* Mulling it over, doing it, enjoying it, regretting it.
- *Accepting the Proposal:* Mulling it over, doing it, enjoying it, regretting it.
- *Gaining Approval from Parents or Loved Ones:* Who knew this could be such a challenge?

> *"The first time I brought my then-boyfriend home to meet my mother, she pulled me aside and said, 'Jeez, he's pretty hairy, isn't he?' She eventually learned to love him."*

> *"I can't wait to get married. The problem is that my mother is giving me a really hard time. She's not wild about my fiancée. I think my mother is genuinely having trouble separating herself from me. I'm worried about what things will be like after we're married. My wife-to-be gets really annoyed with me for placating my mother. I can't allow my mother to come between us, but I don't want to lose her either."*

This isn't a terribly uncommon situation. We'll take a look at this anxiety-producing experience in Chapter 3.

- *Creating a Guest List Without Starting a Family Feud:* You laugh now, but this can be one of the most hair-raising aspects of planning a wedding:

"This was the most difficult part of it. We could only afford to invite a small fraction of the people we wanted. My future in-laws were pressuring me to increase their 'allowance' of invitees. It was pretty tense."

Consider tape recording discussions both of you have together during the wedding planning stages. Record your parents and in-laws discussing the plans with you too. This will help you remember the good times you had planning your wedding.

- *Picking Out Place Settings*
- *Finding a Good Caterer*
- *Finding a Good Photographer*
- *Choosing Between and Finding a Good Band or DJ*
- *Finding, Deciding On, and Renting a Space:*

"I couldn't believe that my wedding date was dependent on the availability of space at the country club."

- *Picking a Wedding Date*
- *Buying a Marriage License*
- *Taking a Blood Test (in some states)*
- *Dealing with Squabbling Relatives and Jealous Friends*

- *Honeymoon Planning*
- *Buying Rings*
- *Invitations*
- *Stamps*
- *Flowers*
- *Keeping Your Parents and Future In-Laws Happy and Involved*
- *Choosing a Wedding Party Without Insulting Friends*
- *Money:* Finding it, spending it, borrowing it.
- *Dealing with Unforseen Disasters*
- *Getting Time off from School or Work*
- *Bridal Shower(s)*
- *Buying a Wedding Dress*
- *Picking Out Dresses/Tuxedos for Members of the Wedding Party*
- *Directions to the Church/Synagogue*
- *Where to Put Uncle Joe and His Stinky Cigar:* Picking the seating arrangements can be more dramatic than you ever imagined!
- *Bachelor and Bachelorette Parties:* see the Focus section "Have a Fun, Safe, Meaningful Bachelor Party" (page 38).
- *Rehearsal Dinner*
- *Packing for the Wedding and Honeymoon*
- *Pictures Before or After?*

As if those concerns weren't enough to think about, there are a variety of other, more potentially unpleasant issues to be resolved. What if the marriage doesn't work out? Why even *think* about it now, during such a happy time?

Overcoming Your New Obstacles

You've found the perfect mate, right? There's nothing that could ever separate the two of you. Well, I hope you're right. But remember,

FOCUS

The Prenuptial Agreement

What is a prenuptial agreement?

A prenuptial agreement is a legally brokered document that may be enforced when and if the two of you divorce, or if one of you should die. In theory, the agreement prevents the other person from inheriting all of your money and property and defines the terms of inheritance. It is an agreement made before marriage that governs the property rights of each person.

Who needs one? Is it strictly for people of means?

A prenuptial agreement is clearly not for everyone. The typical young couple just starting out, both with limited financial resources, won't need an agreement. In general, most agreements are designed for couples where one person may have great wealth that he or she wishes to retain in the event of death or divorce. Also, they can be helpful in cases where both parties have substantial incomes and assets that they want to protect from having to give away. For the most part, people who sign prenuptial agreements have amassed great fortunes, have large family inheritances or family money, or are embarking on second marriages. On the other hand, a prenuptial agreement can offer a certain peace of mind—whether or not you have a lot of wealth to protect.

people get divorced. Some of those failed marriages will happen to friends of yours. Some of those failed marriages will happen to friends of your friends—those friends could be you:

"When my fiancé gently broached the subject of a premarital 'agreement,' I flipped. I told him the only 'agreement' I would make with him

Is a prenuptial agreement necessarily legally binding?

Like many other "sure things" in life, prenuptial agreements don't always work. In order for a prenuptial agreement to be enforceable, many criteria have to have been met. First, both you and your partner must have your own attorneys. The same lawyer cannot, ethically, represent you both. In addition, the contract you establish must be fair and reasonable. That is, the agreement, despite any one-sidedness of wealth, can't completely deprive the financially weaker party of money in the event of divorce or death. Both parties must fully disclose all assets at the time the contract is drawn up, and they must be fair and reasonable at the time of enforcement.

What should I look for in an attorney?

While you'll both need separate representation, you won't necessarily need to retain separate attorneys after the agreement has been finalized. Referrals from trusted friends are a good way to find capable attorneys. The lawyer should feel comfortable with the work being requested of her and must be up-front about her fees.

Be sure to choose an attorney who understands your particular needs and has the time to seriously consider your situation. The attorney should make you feel understood. It's a good sign when you're made to feel as though you're the attorney's only client. She should be dedicated to providing you all the information

(continued on next page)

is where he could stick the paperwork. Where is his confidence in our ability to go on loving each other, even in the face of conflict?"

While nobody ever likes to consider that their bliss might one day be shattered by the rumblings of unhappiness and dissatisfaction, the facts speak for themselves:

(Focus—continued)

you need to make important decisions. You should feel comfortable telling her things you might not be able to disclose to others. A good way to conceptualize the comfort level is to imagine the worst scenario: Would the attorney feel comfortable coming down to the county jail with your bail money?

Can't a prenuptial agreement foster distrust and bad feelings between engaged or married couples?

You betcha. Couples don't like to think that their marriage will fail. Worse yet, who wants to think about the fact that they'll be cut off from their spouse's financial resources if the marriage does fail? Drafting a prenuptial agreement can feel like planning for failure. Who needs the extra stress? But if the two of you, or more typically one of you, feels that an agreement is necessary, it's best to try to put aside your feelings and concentrate on the legal work. On the other hand, no one should feel coerced or railroaded into signing an agreement they're uncomfortable with—especially if there are existing or future children in the picture. You both have your own legal and financial interests. That's why you both need your own representation. The best way to approach any differences of opinion—regarding the prenuptial agreement or issues—is through the time-tested trio of talk, patience, and compromise.

Can an agreement be reassuring to both parties?

Well, clearly for the wealthy party, it offers peace of mind. In fact, for some couples, the party with fewer resources may request an agreement to prove to the wealthier person that he or

- There will be many more than 1 million divorces in the United States this year.

she is not in it for the money. For the party with fewer re-sources, there are some advantages. Remember, an enforceable prenuptial agreement has to be fair and reasonable. In this sense, provided the agreement remains valid, the party with fewer resources will be guaranteed a portion of assets should the marriage end in divorce.

How long is the agreement good for?

Provided that your financial or social circumstances don't change significantly—although they usually do, especially when children enter the picture—a prenuptial agreement is good until death.

How long does it take to complete the agreement?

If both parties are in agreement and have legal representation, the document can be drawn up and signed within a matter of weeks. More complicated issues, such as vast differences of opinion needing to be resolved by your respective attorneys, may take months or longer.

How much does it cost?

Depending on how long it takes to come to a reasonable agreement, and how much your attorneys charge, the cost may be minimal or may be substantial. Negotiations may sometimes drag on for months or longer, increasing legal fees and the overall cost. On the other hand, if you're convinced that a prenuptial agreement is for you, and you're willing to work through the emotional and financial risks, you should be prepared to view your total expenditure as an investment, rather than a one-time expense.

- More than half of all newlyweds will eventually become divorce statistics.

FOCUS

Have a Fun, Safe, Meaningful Bachelor Party

Ah, the traditional bachelor party. Why have one? Well, for one thing, it's something your male siblings, father, uncles, or best friends will want to give you as a sort of "parting gift":

> *"My party was the best part. I felt honored to have so many of my buddies there. We sat around, had a drink or two, and talked about old times. It was terrific."*

Bachelor parties are also a great way to renew old friendships and to include important people in your life. It's also a nice way to blow off some steam before the wedding—a time of great pleasure but also some understandable anxiety. Sometimes, of course, the groom-to-be can get carried away:

> *"I knew my friends were planning a party for me. To be truth-ful, I was a bit nervous. I wanted to have fun, but I wasn't into staying up all night, drinking, being sick, and who knows what else—especially the night before the wedding. Before I knew it,*

In Chapter 10, we'll take a closer look at the social issues related to divorce. What can you do, though, before marriage to protect yourselves financially from the possibility of divorce? A prenuptial agreement is designed to keep you from worrying about painful, difficult-to-manage choices at a vulnerable time. See the Focus section "The Prenuptial Agreement" (page 34), to look at some common questions and concerns to explore whether or not such an agreement makes sense for you.

I was staying up all night, drinking, being sick, and doing who knows what else. It really wasn't what I wanted."

The bachelor party has a rich tradition of being a wild, fun, last-gasp shot at freedom, independence, and the sowing of one's proverbial wild oats. Most parties go off without a hitch. While you should relish the thought of spending time with your old buddies, you should also be wary of irresponsible, excessive drinking, drug use, driving while intoxicated, and sexual impropriety. That said, here's how you can increase your chances of having a great time without encountering the pitfalls:

- *Consider alternatives to the conventional party:* Keep it small and intimate. Have dinner, see a show or movie with your best friends. Stay at home and get out the college yearbook or photo album. Talk about old times together. Remember, it's not what you're doing but the people with whom you're doing it that makes for a great time.
- *Consider a joint bachelor and bachelorette party:* Invite over all your closest friends and enjoy them all together.

(continued on next page)

Being There for Each Other

While full of pleasures and excitement, planning a wedding can also stress the healthiest among us:

"You want stress? After living her entire life without a solitary infectious disease and after planning the wedding meticulously for a year, right

(Focus—continued)

- *Rent a room:* If you do decide to go out, rent a room at a local hotel or use a friend's home or apartment for your fun. The less travel, the better. Avoid bar-hopping.
- *Plan:* Ask your best, trusted friend to plan the evening in advance. Spontaneous bachelor parties can be risky. Stay away from any activities that seem out of the ordinary, and be sure to address any concerns your fiancée might have about your evening.
- *Designate:* Assign a non-drinking driver so that if you or any of your friends need to go anywhere, transportation can be provided safely.
- *Arrange:* Arrange for safe entertainment through a reputable agency. Word-of-mouth is a good way to find good entertainment.
- *Think:* Use common sense and good judgment. Maintain control over your life.
- *Relax and have fun:* You're rapidly approaching the most meaningful day of your life. Rejoice in your good fortune and good friends.

down to what time Aunt Ruth's plane would be landing, my wife comes down with the chicken pox."

Chicken pox aside, as we discovered earlier in this chapter, who wouldn't have moments of anxiety when faced with a list of dozens of things to do—each one of which has numerous possible consequences—some good, some bad? What can you do to make things easier? Well, remember that the two of you are a team. What happens to one will undoubtedly impact the other. You can lessen stress in the relationship by working together to solve problems.

Of course, working together and being there for each other doesn't always mean that the outcome will immediately and inevitably affect you for the better. Sometimes being there for each other means doing things *for others* in a way that will make things easier for both of you. Case in point: the bride-to-be's future mother-in-law:

"I can honestly say that I felt completely excluded from the wedding plans. After all, it's my son who's getting married. I realize that the bride's family needs to do most of the arranging, but I felt quite useless and unappreciated. I told my son. He wasn't pleased with me for butting in. He told his fiancée, who told her parents. They then got all bent out of shape and told my son's fiancée, who told my son, who told me to mind my own business. Everybody started arguing. It was terrible."

It's sometimes hard to remember that wedding plans directly and indirectly include numerous people—some of whom might feel a bit let down. In the example above, the bride's future mother-in-law seemed especially neglected, even estranged. How common an occurrence is this? It happens a lot. How can you include your future mother-in-law, solidify your relationship with her, further endear yourself to your fiancé, and avoid potential conflict? Brides-to-be should check out the Focus section "How to Include Your Future Mother-in-Law" (page 42).

It Just Keeps Getting Better

Wow! So now you have (or almost have) a wife or a husband. As the day arrives, how are you dealing with your excitement and anxiety? How did it feel as you walked (or were strongly encouraged to do so by your family) down the aisle? People's experiences vary wildly. The wedding is an effortless dream-come-true for some:

"I felt like I floated down the aisle. It was the culmination of a lifelong fantasy of mine."

FOCUS

How to Include Your Future Mother-in-Law

Sure, she's not your mother, but she may want to be, at least when it comes to helping with the wedding. She's also "losing" a son—which can rattle even the most stoic mothers. Having a nice working alliance with your future mother-in-law can help smooth a potentially rocky transition—and give you one less thing to worry about. Whether or not you see eye-to-eye with your future mother-in-law, your relationship with each other is inevitable and, you hope, long-lasting. How can you include her in the wedding plans or make her feel useful and included?

- *Rehearsal dinner:* The rehearsal dinner usually happens the night before the wedding and is generally held to feed out-of-town guests and honor the wedding party. Much of the time, it's planned and paid for by the groom's parents. If you're planning to have a dinner, consider getting your future mother-in-law involved right off the bat. Planning a rehearsal dinner involves numerous important issues such as financing, picking a place and time, choosing menus, selecting invitations and a guest list, working out transportation issues,

"*Just what I expected. Beautiful.*"

For others it's a mixed bag:

"*I was nervous. Slightly overwhelmed and mildly nauseated.*"

"*I had an uncontrollable urge to hop down the aisle vigorously, wearing a bunny suit. I was completely berserk.*"

And slightly less dreamlike for others:

and providing directions. Your future mother-in-law should have a chance to help with as many of these details as she likes—especially if she and your future father-in-law are paying for the event.

- *Showers:* Wedding showers are as much a part of marriage as walking down the aisle. Let your future mother-in-law help plan and carry out a shower with your chosen maid of honor.

- *Out-of-town guests:* Ask her if she'd be willing to help you make arrangements for out-of-town wedding guests—pick an appropriate hotel, negotiate a room price, reserve the rooms, and help keep track of the out-of-town guest list. She may also be willing to help in sorting out transportation and special-needs issues for elderly or handicapped guests.

- *Registry:* Ask her to accompany you to the department store to help you decide what items to include on your bridal registry. Keep in mind, this can be a courtesy. You don't necessarily have to follow her advice. She'll probably be happy that you're including her.

- *Treat her to dinner:* It doesn't need to be an expensive or elaborate dinner, but taking your mother and future mother-in-law out to eat is a nice way of including both women in your life.

"With each of my upper limbs being firmly supported by my parents, they gently but firmly carried me down the aisle."

So you finally said "I do," or are about to. What's going through your mind? This event, long planned and eagerly anticipated, arouses such a multitude of feelings—love and warmth as well as anxiety and stress. The feelings may stem from a sense that marriage is so final or that while it means a new beginning, it also signals an end to a chapter in your life. Marriage engenders a multitude of positive and negative feelings.

YOU MAY BE FEELING . . .

In Love   For most couples, the wedding symbolizes the ultimate expression of love and commitment. Up to this point, there's probably been no more powerful event in your lives.

A Sense of Finality   The wedding is the culmination of a great deal of planning, soul searching, and dialogue. For some, it symbolizes a good kind of finality:

> *"My wedding meant the closure of the book of indecision and anxiety. I'm very relieved."*

For others, the finality comes with a hint of ambivalence:

> *"I finally realized that the only sowing of wild oats I could do anymore was with my new wife."*

A Sense of Beginning   As one chapter in your life closes, another new and exciting one begins: your lives together as a married couple.

Thrilled and Ecstatic   The wedding commonly engenders feelings of elation and joy:

> *"It's what I've waited my whole life for."*

Anxious   While feelings of joy are common, couples may also feel nervous about any number of things. Remember, a mixture of feelings is healthy:

> *"While I was ecstatic during the ceremony and afterward, I started thinking about a bunch of things during the honeymoon. I'm worried about the responsibility. How can I provide for my fledgling family?*

What if we fight and we can't resolve it? What if my wife cheats on me? I guess these concerns knocked some of the wind out of the sails of delight for me."

Given all this, how could you not be a bit nervous? Try to remember that a wedding is not part of a typical day in the life of your marriage. As the months pass, you'll have plenty of time to put things in perspective.

> ❧ Try not to resolve your mixed feelings all at once. Give yourself a bit of a respite and enjoy these new experiences and feelings.

Blessed and Fortunate   Many couples count their blessings and feel thankful for having been brought together. A sense of spirituality overwhelms them.

Numb and Overwhelmed   Not terribly uncommon, some can't remember certain parts of the wedding or reception:

"It all seemed like such a blur to me. I don't remember walking down the aisle. What am I? Crazy?"

As often happens with powerful events, couples can easily become overwhelmed by emotion:

"Before the wedding, I was so anxious, I needed a drink to calm me down—and I don't drink. My whole body was shaking. I almost felt like I wasn't there. It was so peculiar. I came back to Earth after we each said 'I do.' But I have very little memory of the whole thing."

Don't worry. Your memory will slowly return. Don't forget that a wedding can be an emotionally and physically exhausting event. Give yourself some time to absorb it.

Underwhelmed   It happens:

> *"I don't see what the big deal is. I really don't."*

A Sense of Anticlimax   After all you've invested over the years, a wedding occupies a rather tiny proportion of that time and before you know it, it's over:

> *"We worked and worked. We picked out those stupid spoons we'll never use, resolved conflicts with relatives, invited people we didn't want, argued, made up, went on with things, got married, went away, came back, and here we sit. Now it's over—all that time, money, and energy."*

Marginalized   Is the experience necessarily a positive one? Some people actually feel left out during and after the wedding—almost like they're not even needed:

> *"There was so much pomp that I felt unnecessary. My new wife was so busy making the rounds that she didn't have a lot of time for me. We had our first fight as a married couple on our wedding night! Can you imagine? If I could do it over, I would insist on a small, intimate gig."*

While the wedding and reception demands that the two of you are spread thin—especially at a large wedding—try to capture each other periodically during the day. Make sure you spend time together talking:

> *"I knew we'd both be busy during the day so we both decided that every twenty-five minutes or so, at the reception, we'd turn to each other, or find each other, and ask each other how we're doing. It worked out great. We both felt comforted by each other, needed, and special—like we had our own little secret club or something."*

⊠ Regardless of how the wedding reception is going, carve out enough time so that you can check in with each other. Talk from time to time and take each other's emotional pulse.

Exhausted Getting married is like running a marathon. The entire weekend is usually filled with all sorts of activities and running around making last-minute arrangements, airport pickups, and so on. Add in some emotional exhaustion, and you'll probably be tired by the end of the day:

> *"There we were. Married. For the first time in our lives, we had the world's permission to have sex. We were both so tired we decided to just go to sleep."*

Whether you have two people, or two hundred people, your wedding day will be unforgettable. Allow for a mixture of feelings—even delighting in the new and sometimes strange feelings a powerful event can elicit. Make sure you talk to each other and try to keep things in perspective. Above all, enjoy the meaning of the event and let yourself be excited about your future together. See the Focus section "Keep Track of Your Married 'Firsts'" (page 48), for a list of ideas.

THE HONEYMOON: YOUR FIRST TRIP AS A MARRIED COUPLE

While the two of you have more than likely traveled together before, there's nothing quite like the honeymoon. There are lots of fun firsts to experience:

FOCUS

Keep Track of Your Married "Firsts"

Your married firsts will make up part of the fabric that binds you together. Try to keep track of as many as you can by writing down important dates or events on your calendar. You'll have a great time recalling them to each other, your families, friends, and children.

- Don't underestimate the importance of your first-month "anniversary." Talk about how your lives have changed. Wherever you are, celebrate the day with an intimate evening and bottle of champagne.

"The first time someone called me 'Mrs.,' I turned around to see if my husband's mother had followed us to the airport—something not completely unexpected. It felt really funny. After all, it's not my name, but it felt so great. We actually registered as 'Mr. and Mrs.' for the first time."

Your honeymoon should be the most carefree, self-indulgent time of your new lives together. Don't worry about your job, money, in-laws, or pesky neighbors. It's a time to love and appreciate each other, think of nothing but yourselves, and relax!

What's so special about the honeymoon? A honeymoon, whether you travel near or far, is really the first statement the two of you make to the world as a married couple. It's a way of announcing who you are and what you're all about. It's also a time to learn more about each other and the ways in which you'll conduct yourselves as husband and wife.

The honeymoon is also the ideal time to relax and recover. Remember, the time surrounding a wedding can be pretty intense. Take some time during your honeymoon to talk about where you've been

- Tape record, or record on your calendar, the first time you refer to each other as "husband" or "wife" in public.
- Pay special attention to your first purchase together as a married couple.
- Make sure all your friends are interviewed on video- or audiotape at the wedding. You'll get a kick out of their comments when you watch the tape year after year.
- Interview each other, on tape, on the plane on your way to your honeymoon destination. What are your future plans? How was the wedding? Any romantic secrets you'd like to share with each other?

together, how you got through it, and where you'd both like to go from here. Of course, you'll have ample opportunity to be intimate and enjoy each other without worrying about the rigors of an ordinary day.

Whatever feelings come up during the honeymoon, one thing is certain: You are celebrating your new life together. Here's how you can make it really special:

- *Don't skimp on romance.*
- *Make dinners together special.* Share a bottle of wine or champagne. Take your time. Enjoy the company!
- *If geography and weather permit, share some intimate sunsets.*
- *Get up early one morning and go to a well-known local spot to watch the sun come up.*
- *Take long, relaxing walks together after dinner.*
- *Treat yourselves to a few things you might not ordinarily do.* Soak in a hot tub, get a massage, enjoy a good book by the pool. Take care of yourselves.

- *Sample the local cuisine together.*
- *If geography permits, rent bicycles or scooters.* Tour the local surroundings and bring a picnic lunch.
- *Stay in the hotel room one evening.* Order room service, talk, eat, drink some champagne, watch a little TV, and go to bed early.
- *Bring a small personal tape recorder with you.* Record the sounds of the beach or mountains. Tape a few of your first casual conversations together as a married couple. Fantasize together about where you'd like to be in a few years, but mostly just enjoy the here and now.

Your Life Together

Getting married. What a great way to spend the day! The culmination of years and months of waiting, thinking, practicing, and discussing has successfully come and gone. The two of you will continue to relive those memories as you make your way together. Get ready for hundreds of new decisions and plans to make, things to buy and enjoy, and fun to have. In the next chapter, we'll look at the complexities of sustaining and nurturing your new marriage and maintaining your relationships with your families.

· 3 ·

Family *Does* Matter

ADJUSTING TO AND ACCEPTING
THE IN-LAWS

3

The fact that you're both new members of each other's families will probably hit you sooner or later. You'll realize that you've both inherited a lot of new family and can look forward to great experiences to come! Great family relationships can actually help the two of you grow closer and fall even more in love. A warm, close, personal relationship with families—your own as well as your spouse's—can provide a sense of security, friendship, and tradition that can form the basis of decades of meaningful experiences:

> *"It's really wonderful just how quickly all of us have bonded. We have a great time together."*

On the other hand, the thought of being forced to spend time with your spouse's family might make swimming in ice water sound attractive. Difficult family issues can rattle the most confident of couples. How can you develop warm relationships and avoid controversy? In this chapter, we'll take a look at some things that go right (and a few that could go wrong) and how the two of you can work together to forge or maintain a positive relationship with your families.

What's New with the Two of You?

It would be difficult to deny that your folks played a major role in your lives. In fact, their influence over you—good, bad, or somewhere in-between—is probably far reaching. If you're like most couples, your opinion of your respective families is largely positive and loving, with a smattering of ambivalence. Despite loving feelings, you may be struggling to find a sense of balance between starting your new life together and maintaining a close relationship with your families. This can be tricky:

> *"My mother is driving us crazy. She's always calling, wanting to visit. I don't know what to say to her. She puts my wife in a strange position— pressuring her to allow a visit. My wife feels uncomfortable with it, but doesn't want to be rude. Then she gets angry at me for not setting limits with my mother."*

In order to have the kind of relationship with your families that feels right, it's important to understand how everybody's life has changed since the two of you got together. Let's start by exploring some of the benefits of great family relations.

ISOLATION

Some family relationships can be complex, but unless you or your spouse have had terrible, or severed, relationships with your families, it's difficult to exist in physical or emotional isolation from them. It's definitely worth the time and effort to make the relationships work:

> *"In looking back over the first few years of my marriage, I really let my family slip away from me—we both did. I was lonely without them, but I thought, for some reason, that it would be best if I separated from them for a while so that I could develop my own sense of who we, as a couple, were."*

You can maintain traditions with your own family while at the same time establishing new ones with your new family. Sometimes sharing holidays can be fun. The experience can also provide each of you with a historical perspective on your spouse's life before you came along.

EQUILIBRIUM

Some people feel that equilibrium is boring and leads to stagnation and a lack of creativity. When it comes to family matters, though, boring can be a blessing:

> *"After months of struggling with my in-laws and parents (receiving spontaneous visits, etc.), we've finally agreed on a plan that will allow everyone to get what they need—some privacy for us and a sense of inclusion for our parents. Perfectly boring. Perfectly perfect."*

CONFLICT RESOLUTION

Over the many years that you'll be married, you'll undoubtedly encounter conflict of one kind or another with your respective families:

> *"My wife's father seemed so distant toward me all of a sudden. It happened just after we got married. I don't get it."*

Learning how to recognize the warning signs and prevent problems is the key to a smooth relationship.

> Recognize that feeling comfortable with your new family takes time. Just because you and your wife have a bond doesn't mean that you and her brother have one.

GRANDCHILDREN
Cultivating positive family relationships now paves the way for good experiences for your unborn children.

ROOTS
Most people like knowing where they came from. They find it meaningful, socially and emotionally, to maintain a good relationship with their families.

PSYCHOLOGICAL NEEDS
Maintaining family cohesion fulfills various emotional needs—gaining approval and admiration; fighting a fear of isolation; and generating advice, love, and closeness, to name a few.

RECIPROCITY
You'll get along best with your husband or wife if you learn together to do things for each other. Learning about your husband's or wife's family will help the two of you grow even closer.

It's clear that working on family issues is important. Having said that, try to remember that uncomfortable feelings elicited by family problems tend to sneak up on you. Very often, it's tough to tell what they're all about. What kinds of feelings develop? Like most relationship issues, the feelings can vary. Feelings are often warning signs that something is amiss, but they can also be an indication that things are going well. Learn to enjoy the pleasant feelings associated with your spouse's family, and pledge to tackle the issues that may sometimes cause friction. Let's take a look at some feelings that can potentially lead to family unity—or stress.

YOU OR YOUR FAMILIES MAY BE FEELING . . .

Happiness   There's no question that the typical, overriding feeling is happiness. After all, your marriage is probably what everybody wanted for you. Most often, your families will be loving, caring, gracious, and giving. What a great way to reinforce your happiness together!

Pride   The vast majority of parents, in-laws, and couples feel enormously proud. To your parents and family members, marriage can often symbolize their success at having raised you well. They'll be brimming with pride.

Closer to Family   For the most part, you and your families will likely be able to capitalize on the positive, loving momentum of the wedding, coupled with your love for each other. You'll all grow closer. Many married couples actually find that their relationships with families improve because of their love for one another:

> *"Who would have guessed that so many diverse people could get along so well? It's great. No problems so far. I've met so many new and interesting people. It's really great. I like my wife, so I guess it figures that I'd like her family too."*

Loss   Nothing gained, nothing lost. How common are feelings of loss? It's often hard to imagine how marriage and the happiness associated with it would lead to such feelings. But many people—including your parents, your in-laws, you, and your spouse—may feel as though you've lost something in the process. This is entirely normal:

> *"I never thought my dad would treat us the way he has. I mean, all of a sudden, he's really protective of me—wanting to know how my new husband is treating me—even though he's known him for years, complaining that he never sees me, and dropping in unexpectedly and without invitation. What's going on here?"*

Mothers and fathers may feel that they've lost a son or a daughter. Recently married men and women may feel that they've lost their old lifestyles, freedom, friends, hobbies, and so on. With communication and compromise you can easily overcome such feelings, which also dissipate with the passage of time.

Emotional discomfort with a sense of loss due to marriage is quite common:

> *"Since our wedding day, I've noticed that my wife seems a bit depressed. Every once in a while, I'll find her crying. She says she can't explain it. She's also been calling her folks daily."*

Separation issues may not be quite so tough to bear if you make your spouse feel as if his or her family is included in parts of your new life.

Ambivalence Feelings are never simply black or white. Positive and negative, clear and unclear feelings often exist side by side. The most emotionally healthy people will usually have a mixture of feelings about a given subject. Likewise, most married couples and their families will probably experience many different feelings after the thrill of the wedding subsides:

> *"I know that my mother, who never really liked my new husband for reasons I don't understand, is in many ways very happy for us—she showers us with gifts and attention. But I've also noticed that she's become, all of a sudden, not too terribly pleasant to my husband's parents. I guess her feelings are pretty mixed up."*

Excluded   Marriage sometimes has a way of making people feel like outsiders. Newlyweds are understandably busy making plans for their future together. In-laws and parents may perceive their children's normal preoccupation with life as a snub or rejection:

> *"Our folks have been trying to see us now for some time. We're both so busy that this just isn't a great time. I got into a huge fight with my parents, and hers, when I tried to explain it to them. Then, my wife and I started arguing because she told me I was rude to her parents. What a mess."*

The end result can be feelings of estrangement and alienation. For married couples, especially during the first year or so, coping with all the demands—being a good husband or wife, calling and visiting relatives, having family over, starting your own traditions, doing things the way you want to do them—can take its toll:

> *"My wife and I are so tired of all the pressures placed on us to be 'dutiful' children to our families. If I forget to send my mother a card for Mother's Day, she's all over me—asking me why I don't love her anymore. I asked my wife to remind me to send a card and she forgot. Now she and I are fighting. It all seems so complicated."*

Competitive   In-law trouble? It happens:

> *"It's really very, very simple. My parents and her parents hate each other. They can't be in the same room together. It's like a zoo full of wild animals."*

Sometimes in-law squabbling can result from, or in, competitive feelings: Who can be the best, closest, most loving parent, for example.

So what's the bottom line? If the feelings are primarily good (with just a smattering of unpleasantness), couples and their families tend to have a pretty smooth first year. What if the feelings are mostly negative? What happens then? As we'll see later on, tension within families will almost always adversely affect the new couple. First we'll look at the causes of conflict in more detail.

Overcoming Your New Obstacles

The two of you may not experience any significant family difficulties. For most of us, our new lives together fill most everyone we know with love, pride, and happiness, with the exception of the occasional argument or misunderstanding. Occasionally, though, conflict can intensify. What can go wrong? Let's take a quick look:

> *"I love almost everything about this man—my husband. I love the way he talks. I love the way he looks. I even love the way he chews gum. I do not, however, love the way he lets his mother come into my house, insult me, compete with me for his affection, and criticize the way I keep my house. When I confronted him about it, he told me that there was absolutely no way he could do or say anything to change her behavior towards me . . . and that he didn't even think it was that bad. We haven't spoken now for two days. The house is very tense."*

> *"Since we got married, my husband all but ignores his mother. Now I'm* his *mother. It's horrible. Now his mother is coming to me for advice.*

She thinks he doesn't love her anymore. The truth is that he'll barely talk to her anymore. I think he thinks that when he married me, he somehow had to give up his mother."

The reasons for family problems—which will usually come back to haunt you if they're not resolved—are varied and complex. However, common themes emerge.

WHAT ARE THE ISSUES?

Getting married often involves complex behavioral changes. The two of you by necessity will focus more on each other than you ever have before. You'll direct most of your energy not at your respective families, but at each other. That's understandable and generally desirable. This important shift can sometimes be a catalyst for the escalation of hidden, dormant, or barely detectable conflict in your families. Consider these possibilities:

Family Secrets Every family has them. Sometimes, you might find out about them before the wedding. Chances are, though, you'll become more involved in or aware of them as the two of you become more involved with each other. Sometimes, your spouse will divulge the secret, but other times both of you may have been kept in the dark and may discover the secret by accident:

"No one ever suspected that my wife's uncle had a serious drinking problem. Believe it or not, it was at the wedding that we finally realized something was wrong."

Some family secrets are simply embarrassing or unpleasant. But sometimes though, they can be more serious. Issues related to sexual impropriety or abuse, mental or medical illness, alcoholism, arrests, domestic violence, drug abuse, and poverty may become more obvious —even shocking. Family secrets don't always present themselves on a silver platter. Most often, the evidence builds slowly, beginning with a suspicion and becoming more obvious over time. Regardless, they tend to affect everyone in the family, including you. Later on in this chapter, we'll take a look at ways to help you cope with this potential unpleasantness.

Competition   Competitive feelings are universal—we all experience them. Arising from personality styles, everyday human experience, envy, adjustment issues, personal insecurities, or lack of manners, such feelings can sometimes develop among members of your new family— and possibly be directed at you. No matter how smoothly things have progressed, there will probably be a time or two when you become embroiled in a competitive situation with a family member. This will be particularly true if your families have a history of being competitive:

> *"My mother has always been very competitive with me, but it's worse now that I have a husband. She always tries to look better than me— more make-up, more expensive dresses, bragging about her travel exploits. It makes me sick. She'll never change."*

Families can exhibit intense competitive behavior. Your new families might compete with each other for your attention and love, or they may even compete with you for a variety of reasons.

An atmosphere of competition is often generated using slights, criticism, jokes, and insults, which may be direct or indirect. Your new mother-in-law might, for example, directly let you know that she thinks she knows better than you how to run the house, how to take care of her son, what foods he likes, how she would man-age things, or that your husband—her son—looks a little too thin. Likewise, your new father-in-law might comment on your line of work and income potential (or lack thereof), how hard it must be for the two of you to get by on your income, or how you can stand to live in such a small apartment.

Some people are more indirect about expressing such feelings. Mothers-in-law might drop in and bring a fully cooked meal, ask to do the laundry, take up your new husband's time, and so on.

> ❧ Don't forget—you're a team. Talk, talk, talk. Listen, listen, listen.

Old Emotional Issues Your parents' or in-laws' emotional issues may sometimes emerge in reaction to your newfound happiness. Periodically, your families may consciously or unconsciously squeeze themselves into your shoes, wish to relive their early years, and may rejoice in or, conversely, resent your happiness:

> *"My parents kind of regressed after I got married. My mother was very needy, sometimes almost resentful of my happiness. It was weird. I didn't know what to do."*

Try to remember that your gain is, in some psychological ways, their loss. Also, while they're undoubtedly proud, your marriage signifies another important milestone in their life cycle. Since it also means they're aging, your marriage may feel bittersweet to them. Just as you've gained new family, your parents and in-laws have too. Whenever many different personalities are thrown together, there's bound to be a time of adjustment.

You Hate Your In-Laws In some cases, you may end up despising your in-laws:

How to Avoid Marital Conflict When Your Family Is to Blame

You won't be able to solve all the problems right away. But you clearly stand the best chance of succeeding if the two of you are secure in your marriage and steadfast in your approach. Here's what to do:

- *Talk:* This works. Meaningful dialogue should be the mainstay of your relationship. Your ability to discuss important issues with your partner will help avoid or work through 99 percent of marital predicaments. How can talking help? By sharing your feelings with your husband or wife about any number of important issues, you can avoid miscommunication, splitting (the playing off of one against the other by another family member), and other potentially disastrous problems. Engaging in meaningful dialogue will also bring the two of you closer together. Make sure you sit down with each other and really talk—without distraction. Take turns talking and listening. Put yourself in each other's shoes.

"Let's see, how can I put this politely? My mother-in-law is the biggest nightmare in the world. I don't understand how my husband turned out so well. I can't stand even being in the same room with her. She's bossy, entitled, demeaning, and whiney. She hates me. My husband teases me about it and reminds me that the apple never falls far from the tree."

Don't worry. You're not alone. Most couples seem able to deal with the episodic crises caused by hostile in-laws, but not without a cost:

- *Compromise:* Another vital method of conflict resolution is compromise. There will be plenty of times when you and your mate won't see eye-to-eye on the significance of an issue. Dialogue and compromise are the best ways to work together to resolve the issues.
- *Humor:* While nobody would expect you to resolve family crises by becoming a stand-up comedian, maintaining a good sense of humor will get you through some tough times.
- *Arrange a time:* Getting together to resolve conflict after it's done its damage is clearly not the best approach. Arrange to get together often to talk—go out for coffee or decide on a time each week when you can sit together and discuss things that are important to the two of you. That way, when a problem does arise, the two of you will already have started talking about it.
- *Solidify the team:* Do whatever you can to shore up your relationship together. Remember, when you're a team, you'll never have to worry about anything by yourself. You'll always travel through the problems together.

"My in-laws are coming for dinner. I think we'll cook them in the big pot and use the large skewers. Seriously, my wife and I are already fighting. I'm trying to think of what I can serve them."

Your In-Laws and Parents Hate Each Other This hatred can also cause a lot of family conflict:

"My husband's parents and my parents can't even look at photos of the wedding without commenting on how miserable the others are."

FOCUS

Enjoy Time with Your Families

What to do first? Make sure you have a solid base on which to address important issues. Remember, by taking care of your relationship with each other, you're far more likely to be able to resolve tough family conflicts.

- *Talk, compromise, humor:* Dialogue must be the foundation of your relationship. That, plus compromise, will help prevent misunderstanding and conflict between you. Don't take yourselves too seriously, and remember that when a problem does arise, the two of you will already have started a process of talking and caring about each other's concerns.
- *You're a team:* Never worry alone. Depend and rely on each other.
- *Politely set clear limits:* It's never easy to tell a loved one that now isn't the best time. But it's important to establish guidelines early on. This is particularly important for the unex-

Boundaries   A boundary is the invisible place where you stop and another person begins. A boundary can be physical or emotional:

> *"I don't like how close my husband's brother sits to me. He also makes provocative comments. It makes me feel very uncomfortable."*

Sometimes, being in a relationship with another person makes people feel entitled, or permitted, to do and say things they ordinarily might keep to themselves. The same holds true for new family members. Boundary violations in a marriage typically center on the unpected and unwanted visits, the unannounced intrusions, frequent phone calls at inappropriate times, and even personal attacks on your husband or wife. Simple statements like, "Gee, Dad, I'd love for you and Mom to come over, but now isn't such a great time. How about Friday at 8?" recognize family members' desires and offer them choices and alternatives.

- *Make your desires clear:* Do your parents and in-laws hate each other? The two of you should work together to politely let your families know that their fighting among themselves is disruptive and unwelcome. If they want to fight with each other, they can do it somewhere else. Tell them it's okay that they dislike each other, but that they should keep it to themselves.
- *Acknowledge their anxieties:* It always helps when family members feel that they're being heard and understood. When the issue of visits comes up, let them know that you understand how much they want to see you. Remind them that you're still their son or daughter and always will be.

(continued on next page)

wanted or unannounced repeated visits from in-laws, a mother-in-law trying to take care of her son, and similar situations.

Sometimes, a variety of other boundary issues arise. "Splitting," for example, might happen if your mother comments to you that your new wife, who burned the turkey the other day and accidentally threw out all of your socks, doesn't seem ready to handle being married, and that she was rude to your mother the other day. This might result in a fight between you and your new wife. The victor? The mother of course. She's managed to split the two of you apart to fulfill her own

(Focus—continued)

- *Look at yourselves:* Ask yourselves some important questions. Are we being reasonable? Whose conflict is this? Is there any way we could make things go more smoothly? Remember, nothing is ever black or white. There's always room for uncertainty and ambivalence. Sometimes, conflict arises not from one party or the other, but from the way in which the parties interact. Ask a friend who's been married for some time for an objective second opinion.
- *Be forgiving:* The first year of a marriage is an incredibly important and often complicated time for everyone involved. Despite any rocky beginnings, things have a way of working out. Don't worry if you have to let a few things slide. The first year is an adjustment for everyone!
- *Keep family involved:* Sometimes, the more you resist, the worse things become. Your families will resent your attempts to keep them out of your lives.

psychological needs. Splitting, in this case, might never have happened if your mother did a better job of honoring boundaries. That is, if she kept her thoughts to herself.

Religious Stress This is a particularly dicey topic if husband and wife are of different faiths. Families can sometimes pressure you to be more, or less, active in your faith. And nothing works people into a lather like a religious debate at the dinner table. Try to avoid such arguments at all costs.

Geography So how come you never visit your family? Is it because you live 2,000 miles away and can't afford to take time off from work? Might be.

Here are some more ideas for keeping parents and in-laws happy and involved in your life.

- *Schedule regular visits:* Arrange for set days and times to meet with your parents and in-laws.
- *Have a dads' or moms' day:* Arrange for a day out with all the men and all the women.
- *Go through your parents' wedding albums with them:* You'll be surprised how much you'll learn!
- *Start your own family traditions:* Dinner out once a month (or dinner at your place, then at both sets of in-laws' homes).
- *Schedule a trip together.*
- *Arrange for a yearly photo opportunity.*
- *Have a family reunion with both sides once a year.*
- *Don't forget:* If family members feel they're being included in your lives, they're far less likely to act out their anxieties with you in a less desirable fashion.

Shift in Priorities The inevitable changes in the way you do things will likely affect your families:

> *"I forgot to send my mother a card for Mother's Day. She'll never forgive me. I suppose I'm out of the will."*

So what might be the result of all these complicated issues, problems, and conflicts? Well, for one thing, you can be sure that your relationship with your respective families will suffer a little. More important, though, the two of you will feel stress within your relationship. See the Focus section "Enjoy Time with Your Families" (page 66), for ideas on how to handle these problems.

Being There For Each Other

Okay, so you're bothered by the goings on among your respective family members. The stress is killing you. Your mother-in-law just brought over some new detergent for you to try so you can *finally* start getting the clothes *really* clean, or your in-laws arrived—unannounced—seconds before you and your spouse were about to spend a few intimate moments together. The tension is rising. How can you protect your marriage from such insults? Take a deep breath and consult the Focus section "How to Avoid Marital Conflict When Your Family Is to Blame" (page 64).

It Just Keeps Getting Better

There's nothing more rewarding than having a warm, loving relationship with your respective families. For most couples, such a relationship is well within reach:

"We've actually just started traveling with my in-laws. We love it! They're warm and generous. Every once in a while there's a little friction, but nothing we all can't handle."

For the most part, having a new family can be extraordinarily rewarding and enriching.

Your Life Together

Happily, most relationships with mate's families develop quite smoothly. Working together to repair fractures in your family structure will pay off over time. Try to be sensitive to each other's issues and never lose your collective senses of humor. Do your best to approach family problems with patience and understanding. By talking to each other and employing compromise, you'll be setting the stage for a lifetime of happiness.

· 4 ·

Money Issues

MAKING IT THROUGH
THE FINANCIAL RELATIONSHIP

4

It's never too soon to start thinking about and discussing money. Being married means that there are two of you now—and who knows how many more to come? The dynamics of your lives have changed. It's more important than ever to start saving for your future together and considering impending expenses—like children, or a new home. We all know that thinking, and especially talking, about money matters can be tough. Why? For one thing, we often unconsciously link money with individual self-worth. And who wants to talk about *that*?

The way you approach saving money, financial matters, resolving money problems, and working through tough money questions reflects the way you work together as a team. The two of you *must* openly discuss the intimate details of your finances (if you haven't already). Like it or not, your approach to finances is another important factor in the success of your marriage. In this chapter, we'll look at these important and sometimes difficult issues. We'll also look at some solid ways to build a healthy nest egg.

What's New with the Two of You?

Money-related issues have a way of sneaking into relationships from the start. Just because you're married doesn't mean that you haven't already had some lively discussions about money. This is particularly true if you've lived together for any great length of time:

> "Whenever I dated, it was always interesting to see which one of us was going to pay for dinner or a movie. Of course, as my then-boyfriend and I started to get more serious with each other, the money issues got more complicated."

How complicated?

> "We actually had a lot of tough money problems early on in our relationship. I remember that after my girlfriend and I had been together for about six months, she started wanting to know how much I made, what I did with my money, and so on. We went away together once and she wanted me to pay for everything."

> "Even after we entrusted each other to live together in monogamy, my then-boyfriend (now ex-husband—we've come full circle) was a cheap jerk. Everything was separate. I wasn't allowed to touch his mail or see any of his bank statements, even by accident. He was really possessive and paranoid. After we got married, it continued—separate checkbooks, stamps, bills. Ridiculous. I wanted to pool our resources and he felt very uncomfortable with that—even though I suspected we each made around the same amount of money."

Like the ups and downs of love, money can make us feel great about the world, but it can also complicate our lives in ways that are usually avoidable. What are some of the common feelings elicited by finances and money?

YOU MAY BE FEELING . . .

Comfortable, Confident, and Carefree   Most couples are able to negotiate their way through the perils and pleasures of finances without any major upheavals:

> *"We had no problems. We talked and discussed all the issues. It worked out very nicely. If you really love and respect each other, there's very little that can't be worked out."*

Most often, you can overcome any mixed or uncomfortable feelings. The vast majority of couples do a good job dealing with the other person's financial situation. For many couples, a feeling of certainty, equality, and reassurance is common:

> *"I don't really care what our situation is. Whatever happens, I know we'll work it out. I'm sure that we'll make it."*

Motivated and Ambitious   Marriage can spur creativity and a strong work ethic:

> *"Since I got married, I've become far more interested in making money, saving, and building our lives together. It's a true partnership for me."*

Uncertain About the Future   There's nothing like money to make you feel hopeless, helpless, anxious, and insecure. Such feelings might include fear of not having enough money, trusting your spouse with your money, worries about job security and your financial future as a couple, and confusion:

> *"Who's supposed to buy all the new furniture for our apartment? Do I pay for long-distance calls to my friends? What about gas for the car? Should I keep my own checking account?"*

Negative   Resentment over having to share your money and possessions with your spouse also are common:

"What a large adjustment for me to think that a previous stranger will now know and even possess some of my prized things. I admit that I was pretty guarded about what was mine and felt a bit violated about the whole money thing."

> 🔲 To calm your anxiety, don't invest until you have a cash reserve of three to six months' living expenses.

Sometimes, especially when there's a large disparity between your financial positions, the word "cheap" can creep into the dialogue:

"I want to protect what used to be mine."

"I came into the marriage with very little and don't make all that much money. I certainly don't want to take his money to buy a present for him, but what choice do I have? I bought him a present. He thought the gift was pretty cheesy and inexpensive. It was. I feel so cheap."

Anger can often result from feelings of financial inequity:

"I feel bad. My wife's as poor as a church mouse. When I inherited her, I also got all of her debt. Her father must be laughing his rear-end off."

When one spouse comes into the marriage with more wealth than the other, jealousy sometimes results:

"You'd think I'd be thrilled that my wife's family is wealthy and that she's got a nice trust fund and that we'll never want for anything ever. Yet I'm filled with a certain sense of envy and dismay."

What a variety of feelings! Throughout the chapter, we'll look at ways in which you can capitalize on the positive ones and creatively transform your worries into great experiences.

It Just Keeps Getting Better

In the best situation, newlyweds are not overly anxious or preoccupied with their financial situation. But you should periodically put your heads together about a few things anyway. Your marriage will be far more comfortable if you don't need to worry about where your next meal will come from. Even if one or both of you is wealthy, discussing and reviewing these issues will help you work better together in other areas. Although you may have differences of opinion, being on the same financial wavelength about certain issues is crucial. In the Focus section "Financial Goals: A Checklist" (page 78), we'll explore some desirable financial goals as well as some of the many reasons to have a solid financial working relationship with your spouse.

Being There for Each Other

Up to this point, much of what you have probably been concerned about as a couple has been the wonderful novelty of being married—how to adjust to your new situation, how to stop your husband from snoring, whose turn it is to burn dinner, and so on. You have focused on the here and now.

Many recently married couples are having so much deserved fun together that they're not thinking about the future. But couples may establish patterns early on that can come back to haunt them. An example? Too many couples make a conscious or even unconscious decision not to save money. Citing various reasons—they can't afford to save, it's

FOCUS

Financial Goals: A Checklist

- *Conflict:* One of your priorities should be to minimize money conflict. Money has a way of turning peace-loving people into Wall Street terrors. You can avoid many intense arguments if the two of you share some common ideas about money. Establishing a pattern for spending, saving, investing, and talking about money early on will help you avoid intense conflicts later on.
- *House:* Next to taxes, your single most substantial expenditure likely will be purchasing a home together—if that's in your future plans. Unless you're lucky enough to come into a lot of money for reasons other than hard work, saving for your first home together requires a team approach. You and your spouse must both work, save, talk, and exercise solid judgment.
- *Baby:* The two of you will have to work together in a very specific way to make this happen. But planning for a child, while an exciting and wonderful time in your lives, nonethe-

too time consuming to choose a retirement plan, or that they don't have a head for numbers. Do you need piles of money to be happy? Most people don't. But saving money now can help you achieve financial goals and peace of mind as you grow older.

Saving for the future, unlike the immediacy of getting dinner on the table, is an abstract concept. Issues related to saving money often

less requires some financial planning—something you can't do if you're not planning ahead together.

- *Vacations:* There's nothing more liberating than taking time off together after a lengthy run of misery at your respective places of employment. You'll need a good financial plan to travel on your own terms—where, when, and how often you'd like.

- *Funding your near future:* Who wants to think about financial life years down the road? Instead, think of your future together as next week, the week after, and next year—not necessarily the next decade. Planning for retirement is important, but you've got to think about your near financial future too.

- *Fun:* You should be able to fund fun—not years down the road, but now. Saving for your future is essential, but try not to miss out on fun during the formative years of your marriage.

- *Security blanket:* Should an unforeseen disaster happen to make one or both of you unable to work, the two of you

(continued on next page)

frighten people. They may feel that a tenuous financial status is somehow connected to their worth as people. Some couples don't have the confidence to save. But financial matters, and saving in particular, don't have to be taboo and they shouldn't be mysterious, scary, or dangerous. In the next few sections, we'll identify some problem areas and discuss ways you can continue to enjoy life and safeguard your financial futures.

(Focus—continued)

should have money enough to live on for at least three months.

- *Retirement:* Seems like a long way off. Why start now? As we'll see later on, if the two of you start a modest savings plan now, you'll be multimillionaires by the time you're old enough to retire.
- *Financial freedom:* Having complete control of your financial lives is something most people strive for but rarely achieve. While other issues are essential to a complete, healthy, and happy life, financial freedom can vastly improve the quality of your life together.

We'll look more closely at these important goals, and how to reach them, later. Remember: Couples who work together achieve the best results. It's teamwork—not dumb luck—that determines the financial success of your marriage.

QUESTIONS AND ANSWERS

About Saving Money

Q: *I make pennies. How can I possibly save anything?*

A: Pennies are good! Here's an interesting test: If you were given the opportunity to deposit a penny today and then told that for the next month the previous day's money would be doubled, would you accept a gift of $1 million immediately, or take your chances, wait until the end of the thirty days, and take the result of the penny-doubling offer?

Believe it or not, you'd be foolish to take the $1 million. No kidding. Do the math and you'll find that the penny doubling would leave you with $10,737,418 in pennies, which you could take to your nearest bank and redeem for paper money. It's true. How can this help you? Well, it means that if you play your cards (or pennies) right, you could end up with a small fortune.

Q: Both our families are loaded. What do I care how much money we save? Someone else appears to be doing it for us.

A: I'd hate to know that my financial future was completely dependent on someone else. Relationships change, family fights have resulted in disinheritance, and families sometimes try to influence or even control potential beneficiaries with money.

The discipline of saving money now will help the two of you assume far more responsibility for your lives. Family money is nice to fall back on during times of crisis, but for now it's a good idea to pretend it's not there.

Q: We have a lot of stress. Job problems, family issues. I feel like we're not really grounded yet. Why should we start to save now? We're both very young. Why can't we just start some other time? You know, when we both have our feet on the ground.

A: While it's okay to live in the here and now, the reality is that as you grow older together, you'll have more expenses—kids, cars, college tuition, weddings, etc. By the time your kids are ready for college, the costs could exceed $250,000. The best plan of action for all your future expenditures is to start saving, through careful investment.

Take advantage of your youth. There are astounding benefits to an early savings plan. If you waited five years after your wedding and then started to save $200 per month at 10 percent for fifteen years, you'd have amassed $83,585. However, if you started to save $200 per month

FOCUS

Savings Checklist

Your courtship, engagement, wedding, and ongoing romance are great examples of fabulous personal investments you made in each other. Dealing with financial issues, while not as exciting, can nonetheless be as personally rewarding. Here's what to do:

- *Don't delay.* Begin your savings plan today.
- *Talk.* Your decisions about money need to be made together, as a team.
- *Learn about different investment options.* Start thinking about your options together. What kinds of investments seem to suit both of you? Try to pick the kinds of investments that suit your needs and philosophy. While not a substitute for reading about money or discussing the issue with a trusted adviser or financial planner, here are a few of the many different kinds of investment vehicles.

at 10 percent the very year of your marriage, after twenty years you will have amassed $153,139.

Why wait? If you start now, you'll have the best chance of reaching your financial goals.

Q: I've always been great with money. When we're a little older, we'll start to save. I'm pretty sure I can come up with some way to save. The stock market maybe?

Mutual Funds Mutual funds are simply collections of stocks, bonds, or other similar securities that are nurtured and watched over by a professional money manager. The advantages of mutual funds? Mutual funds allow you to invest small—even tiny—amounts of money without having to study each security or spend a lot. Since professionals manage these funds, you don't need to sleep next to a stock ticker either. The manager will do that.

If you're investing for the long-term—and you should be—and won't be needing your money for a long time, stock mutual funds are generally the way to go. If you're going for long-term growth and savings, remember that even with market downturns, corrections, and crashes, stocks have produced the best overall returns over time.

Savings Bonds Savings bonds are essentially IOUs that are issued to you by the government in return for lending it money. In exchange, the government promises to pay you back with interest. The interest you receive upon redemption is not

(continued on next page)

A: Trusting their sage-like powers to forecast the future (and perhaps forgetting that they may be confronted with unexpected expenses), some people have wildly unrealistic attitudes. Try to remember that the accumulation of wealth requires small investments made regularly over long periods of time. Starting now will give the two of you the greatest chance of having what you need as you grow older. Trying to hit the right stock, years after you should've started a disciplined saving plan, is foolhardy.

(Focus—continued)

subject to state or local taxes. You may be able to redeem savings bonds tax-free if they will be used for your unborn children's college education. Bonds are simple to purchase—visit your local bank to find out more—and are issued in many denominations. They are extremely safe. The big disadvantage is a rather skimpy yield.

CDs and Bank Savings Accounts Certificates of deposit (CDs) and bank savings accounts are practically risk-free savings options. The downside is an abysmal yield. In fact, interest barely keeps pace with inflation. While you may want to keep several months' living expenses in one of these accounts, you don't want to use them for long-term savings. Why? Take a look and decide for yourself:

- $50 invested each month for eighteen years at bank rates of 5 percent will yield $17,533.
- $50 invested each month for eighteen years at 10 percent (the typical long-term stock mutual fund yield) would yield $30,278.

Q: We have everything we need right now. Jobs, food, each other, and an apartment. I'm not into this money thing. What else could we possibly want?

A: How's this: vacations, children, clothes, food and toys for your children, health insurance for your family, a house, cars for you and your kids, college, weddings for your kids, gifts for your grandchildren, and retirement without worry.

Individual Stocks   So exciting—so risky. Buying individual stocks in a particular company is great fun—especially if you know what you're doing. But most of us don't have a clue. *Unless you spend many hours researching the market and the companies in which you're investing, it's a good idea to leave individual investing to the experts.* Don't put your savings in jeopardy. If you must try your hand at individual investing, be sure to employ a reputable broker. Otherwise you're much less likely to do well and build a savings that you can rely on in the future.

Bonds   Bonds are loans you make to an organization—local, state, or federal government, foreign countries, or companies—in return for repayment with interest. Bonds come in many different forms—municipal, long-term, short-term, corporate, government, foreign, junk, and so on. Some are safe, some are not. Unless you're an expert at buying and selling bonds, I'd avoid them at this point in your savings plan. If you're interested in bonds, there are a multitude of varying types of bond mutual funds. Seek the advice of a trusted adviser or broker before you proceed.

(continued on next page)

Q: We barely have enough money to buy food and clothing. How do you expect us to save imaginary money we don't have?

A: Many newly married couples mistakenly feel that saving requires enormous amounts of cash. They often cite lack of financial resources as an excuse not to save. The good news is that the two of you don't need to save tons of money to be successful. Couples with very little money or low current earning potential can save for the futures. Take a look:

(Focus—continued)

- *Choose an investment vehicle.* Your best bet, if you're aiming for long-term growth, is to invest in a stock mutual fund. Remember, professionals manage stock mutual funds, relieving you of any serious market study; these funds can be purchased in minute quantities to suit your particular financial status; and over the long haul they provide superior returns. Try not to worry too much about your foray into the market.

  Remember that the stock market will fall sometimes. However, because yours is a long-term investment, your mutual fund will more than likely recover. In fact the market always recovers in time. A market correction also gives you the opportunity to buy more of the stock mutual fund at a lower price.

  There are many different kinds of stock mutual funds— growth, aggressive, small company, global, and so on. If you feel nervous about the risk, consider an index fund—one that mirrors the overall performance of the stock market.

- $100 invested each month for forty years at 10 percent would yield $637,678.
- $200 invested each month for forty years at 10 percent would yield $1,275,356.
- $500 invested each month for forty years at 10 percent would yield $3,186,390.

While you still might not have enough to travel around the world, you still have many options. For example, if you're eventually able to

- *Contact a mutual fund company.* Stick with one of the better known, highly rated companies. Call and ask an adviser to recommend a fund that has either kept up with the market or has exceeded it. Ask them to send you literature on the funds.

  Whether or not you decide to have joint or separate savings accounts will depend on a number of important issues: how the two of you approach money, whether you pool your income, your tax situation, whether you file taxes jointly or separately, and so on. Ask your accountant for advice and read on for more on pooling.

- *Max out on your ability to contribute to an individual retirement plan, SEP, Keogh, or 401(k) plan.* Why? Consider the tax-deferred (sheltered) interest. Take a look at these figures:

  Dump $2,000 at 10 percent into an IRA at the beginning of every year and after forty years you'll have amassed $1,111,974. If you both contribute a total of $4,000 each year you'll stockpile $2,223,948 after forty years. Nice chunk of change, no?

(continued on next page)

buy a home with your savings, you can take out a home equity loan or line of credit. And if you've saved wisely, you'll need to borrow far less money from other sources.

Q: I'm a here-and-now guy. My wife likes to save. My feeling is that there are too many things I want to do with what little money I have. Why should I give it away by saving?

A: Who's giving it away? It's still yours. Sometimes it's tough for young married couples to see beyond their own current needs or desires.

(Focus—continued)

• *Arrange for automatic debit.* Pretty bad at bookkeeping? Don't worry. Companies are now better than ever at collecting your hard-earned money. When you fill out your mutual fund application, indicate that you'd like a certain monthly amount automatically deducted from your checking account. It's that easy. This way, you'll never need to remember to send in the money. Having the same amount debited from your checking account each month is called "dollar cost averaging" and it allows you to buy more shares of a stock when the price is lower and less of the stock when the price is high.

• *Once you've invested in a fund, ignore it.* Don't pinch it, touch it, squeeze it, sell it, or even look at it. Market swings are normal. Don't fret. Ignore the naysayers and doomsday predictions. Call the mutual fund company once a year to ask if the fund is performing as well as other funds in its class. If it is, leave it alone. If it's not, consider moving your money into a fund that has managed to keep pace a bit better.

• *Consult an accountant.* If you're interested in learning about other more complicated but possibly more suitable forms of saving plans, trusts, or investments, consult an accountant or attorney who specializes in estate planning.

Saving wisely means saving small amounts over many years—a plan that shouldn't interfere with your desire to spend money on yourself.

Q: To me, saving money means competing with the big boys. You know, in the stock market. It's just too competitive for me. Frankly, investing frightens me, and my wife wants me to be cautious. I'm as scared of the stock market as I am of my wife's meat loaf. I don't understand her meat loaf and don't eat it. Why should I invest in something I don't understand?

A: You shouldn't. But it's unfortunate that a lack of confidence may prevent couples from starting to save. Keep in mind that millions of inexperienced savers have successfully put together large nest eggs by investing small amounts, steadily, in mutual funds. We take a look at this savings vehicle in the Focus section "Savings Checklist" (page 82).

> Don't chase after mutual funds that have the greatest one-year return. Invest in one fund and stick with it. Over the long-term, you'll do fine.

Q: *Investing is far too risky. Isn't there some other way?*

A: If you want steady financial gains, you will have to invest in the stock market. You can diminish your risk by investing in mutual funds. Stock market losses, corrections, and even crashes are to be expected and, at times, are even welcome. Don't forget that you're saving money over the long haul and you can afford to weather expected stock market downturns. For long-term gains, only the stock market will give you the returns you need to finance your future.

Q: *How can I save when I have so little time?*

A: Between your job and raising your family, it's difficult to find the time to invest your savings wisely. Lucky for us busy people, more than ever before mutual fund companies make it easy for savers with little or no time to worry about the ups and downs of the market.

FOCUS

How to Identify and Resolve Money Conflicts

- *Identify the problem:* As we've seen, money problems come in all sorts of shapes and sizes:

  "My husband keeps a list of everything he buys for us and everything I buy for us. At the end of the month, he tallies it up."

  "We've always maintained our own accounts and that's the way I want it to stay."

  "When you get married, you should take a leap of faith and plummet headfirst into joint accounts."

  What kinds of problems arise? All kinds:

- *Who buys what?* For couples who elect to keep their money separate, conflict may arise when purchases are reduced to a microscopic level.
- *To combine or not to combine?* Sure, you combined your albums, tapes, and compact discs, but money is an entirely different story. A problem arises when it's determined that

Q: *I have a bit of extra money to invest for us and to pass down to our kids. Fifty dollars per month seems like such a small amount of money, though. Do you think I can start saving with that small amount?*

A: I wish someone had saved $50 a month for me. Consider the results of this unbelievable calculation:

there's an inequity, such as when one person makes more money than the other or one person spends too much.

- *Who pays the bills?* How do the two of you organize your financial responsibilities? Do you share them? Must they be shared? Should you both contribute to every expense?

- *Whose name appears first on joint checks?*

  "My name always went first on the check. Actually, my name was the only name on the check. I like the way my name looks on a check. I don't want to share."

- *Who owns what?*

  "If I pay for something—a big purchase—whose is it really?"

- *Is one partner secretly saving money separately from the joint accounts?*

  "She's got money she's not even telling me about."

- *Is one partner spending impulsively?*

  "I make all the money. He spends it all on dumb grown-up toys like stereos and tires."

- *Who's in control?*

(continued on next page)

Thanks to compound interest, if you invested $50 per month at 10 percent for only eighteen years, then *never* contributed another dime, in sixty-eight years, your heirs would have a nest egg of $4,401,569! That's the result of your saving a total of only $10,800 over eighteen years! Amazing.

> *(Focus—continued)*
>
> *"I have to do the checkbook and balance it—to the penny. I need to be in control of where the money goes."*
>
> Once you've identified the problem, use the following strategies to resolve them.
>
> - *Have a team philosophy:* No matter what you as a couple do with your money, you're in this together. Does this mean you have to agree on every issue? Hardly. It means that you can sit in two different chairs, but look out over the same horizon together.
> - *Discuss everything:* Talk with your spouse about your financial fears, concerns, and goals.
> - *Take things one at a time:* Resolve not to solve all the issues at once. Start with the simplest and easiest issues. Table the remainder. Enjoy the incremental resolution.
> - *Accept your differences:* If relevant, accept the fact that one of you may make more than the other. But be sure to discuss how it affects both of you emotionally.
> - *Choose between joint or separate finances—or both:* Try to resolve the issue of "joint" versus "separate" finances early on. Many couples with two paychecks choose to combine all their money, while others tend to prefer separate accounts. This can be tricky and

Q: We never have enough money. It leads to big problems in our relationship. What can we do?

A: Read on.

There are, of course, important tax implications for your savings. Your financial planner or accountant can help you manage the tax issues. Nonetheless, starting to save now will make those taxes look like pocket change in the long run.

tends to lead to conflict—especially if one paycheck is bigger than the other. Whether or not you combine your money in a single checking account is a matter of preference and depends on how well you can work together to come to an acceptable resolution.

Many couples have both. That is, they have a joint account for basic necessities and separate accounts for everything else. Other couples closely track expenses and, depending on incomes, will spend money as a percentage of their income. No matter what separate funds you might keep, it's a good idea to have at least a small joint checking account.

Regardless of what you decide to do now, keep in mind that as you grow together, who spends how much on what will likely become less important. You'll both contribute to the well-being of the relationship in numerous ways—ways that transcend finances.

- *Discuss all major purchases:* This is especially important if the purchase is being made with someone else's money. Do not set your husband or wife up for a rude surprise. No surprise credit card statements or depleted savings accounts. Bad feelings and marital discord are often the products of poor judgment—made much worse when a spouse is surprised with the news or finds out accidentally.

(continued on next page)

Overcoming Your New Obstacles

Money is both a powerful force and a symbol. As a matter of fact, money issues frequently are at the root of major arguments during the first year of marriage. The reality is that the both of you, while similar in many ways, have different ideas and attitudes about a lot of things. Nobody sees eye-to-eye on everything:

(Focus—continued)

- *Use your individual talents:* When deciding who should do what (balance the checkbook, buy groceries, pay bills, and so on), try to determine who's best suited for each job. Some people couldn't care less whether the checkbook balances and so are terrible at making sure it gets done. Others, with their calculators always at hand, insist on balancing it monthly—and to the penny. Some get a feeling of accomplishment from paying bills, while others would rather wash the car or do the grocery shopping.

- *Compromise:* When approaching a tough impasse, remember one thing you can always agree on: the importance of finding common ground.

- *Consult:* Draw on the experience of trusted peers. Seek out friends or relatives who have many more married years under their belts than you do and talk with them about how they have resolved money issues. If your issues seem too complex, consider meeting with a financial planner.

- *Meet monthly:* Schedule a meeting with each other once a month to go over tough financial questions, big bills, large expenses, and your savings plan. This is especially important if one of you isn't terribly keen on money issues. Even if one partner hates to think about finances, he or she still should be involved and aware of money matters. Above all, remember that managing—and spending—your money as a couple can be fun. Have fun.

"Until we put our money together, everything seemed idyllic. Then we started to squabble about who was working more, contributing more to the pool of money, how to save, and so on. What a mess."

FOCUS

Romance Update: Finances Can Have Sex Appeal

- *Once every month, bundle up all your expenses, receipts, and bills.* Pack a picnic lunch and a bottle of wine. Have a financial picnic lunch in a remote, romantic spot—your favorite park perhaps. Kill three birds with one stone: Pay the bills, have a delicious lunch, and share some romance.

- *Hold a money contest.* Make it fun to track expenses and expenditures. At the end of the month, each of you must guess your total joint expenses. Tally them up. Whoever comes closest gets a massage and dinner.

- *Share a future-planning session by candlelight.* Have a quiet, romantic dinner together. Discuss your financial hopes, dreams, and plans.

"He keeps saying 'We'll use my money for this and your money for that.'"

"So how do we decide whose name goes first at the top of the checks?"

Money makes us all feel powerful, but when the dollar is causing fights between you and your husband or wife, it's clear that it also has a way of rendering us powerless. In the Focus section "How to Identify and Resolve Money Conflicts" (page 90), we take a look at some common money problems and explore ways to avoid them.

Your Life Together

From that first envelope an older relative tucked into your pocket at the wedding to your first joint account to your third bounced check, money issues will continue to challenge and delight the two of you. Keep in mind that each new money-related issue will be a learning experience for both of you. Make some plans, establish some financial routines, and have fun! Managing your money as a couple will help bring the two of you closer together.

· 5 ·

Making It Legal

PROTECTING YOURSELVES BY
PLANNING AHEAD

5

You've taken steps to help secure your financial future together. What more is there to do? You obviously love and care about each other—that's what all this is about! You show your love and respect for each other every day through dialogue and romance. But there are other ways to show your love. As we've seen, tending to your financial future is one. Another equally important way to show your love is to educate yourself about a variety of legal issues—and take steps to protect yourselves and your future family in the event of a crisis.

You should consider issues like wills, life insurance, and other potentially dull but extremely important concerns as part of your overall plan for the future. Nobody likes to think about death, devastating illness, or disability, but these things happen. Like everything else the two of you will accomplish during the first year, establishing a pattern of responsibly addressing tough issues early on will strengthen your marriage and future family. How? If you take what little time is required now to address these issues now, it's one fewer thing you'll need to worry about later. Today's responsible decisions can influence future generations:

"I know that saving for my future family is important. But what if I wasn't around to make sure everything I want for my family got done? Who would take over? I have a lot of important questions—stuff that I unfortunately wasn't able to learn from my dad."

In this chapter, we'll examine some issues that can be tough to talk about but should still be addressed. We'll explore some of the unpleasantness associated with life—death, illness, and disability—and what you can do to protect yourselves. We'll touch on several ways to prepare for these obstacles, but you should consult a professional for more detailed advice.

What's New with the Two of You?

So, it's settled. You've read Chapter 4, started saving, and the two of you plan to reap the benefits of untold millions and live happily ever after. Right? It sure would be nice, but keep in mind that saving money is not the only way to secure your future. Unforeseen disasters can wipe out your savings sooner than you may realize. What kinds of disasters?

"My husband hurt his back at home and can't work. We're having a tough time supporting ourselves. I've had to get a second job, and I'm so stressed out that we're fighting with each other. I wish there was another way."

Surrendering your hard-earned money to others can be heartbreaking. You can imagine numerous scenarios. What would happen to your spouse if you suddenly passed away or were severely injured? If you're like many newly married couples who already have a child, what would happen if you became disabled and couldn't provide for your family? If you and your spouse died in an accident, who would guarantee your baby's financial future or attend to his or her emotional well-being?

Many people prefer not to think of such unpleasantness, but death and illness do occur, even early on. Disabling illnesses that rob you of your livelihood, vitality, or productivity occur as well. Although you may feel—and actually be—young and vigorous, there's a chance that you might die or become impaired long before your time. Most people recognize this, but some couples stubbornly resist taking the appropriate steps. Why? Let's take a look at other reasons people give for failing to protect themselves later on. As we'll see, the resistance is usually based on emotion:

You May Be Feeling . . .

Superstitious Sometimes people are afraid that talking about something will make it happen. Simply put, many of us are superstitious. Get over it. It ain't so.

Afraid of Losing Your Spouse It's very scary to imagine life without your husband or wife. Who wants to? It's terrible to consider that you may one day be single again. The truth is it happens to just about everybody sooner or later. Most of us will someday become widows or widowers. Accept it and take responsible steps to prepare yourself.

Afraid of Death You may be afraid of death and anything associated with it. Those who say they're not fearful of dying often aren't

> Make provisions for your spouse's and your deaths while you're both alive. Don't complicate your eventual loss by being unprepared.

telling the truth—or they're not admitting their fear to themselves. Try not to let your fear get in the way of planning ahead. If you can, separate your fear from the rest of you and focus on being as businesslike as you need to be to get the job done.

Hesitant to Confront Your Own Mortality   This is understandable. Try to remember that you'll probably live to be at least eighty. Concentrate on doing what you need to do to secure your and your family's future, and then forget about it. Drawing up a will, buying insurance, and so on, will only require periodic review—not daily preoccupation.

As a couple, you should take as much control of your financial situation as you possibly can. Take some time now to protect your family from certain unpleasant possibilities. If you don't, no one else will. Let's take a look at some important and common questions that young people often have when confronted with what seem like "grown-up" problems. Then we'll explore some of the steps you should take as a couple.

QUESTIONS AND ANSWERS

About Wills, Insurance, and the Future

Q: My husband and I are young, active people. We've never been sick a day in our lives. We seem invincible. Does it really pay to spend all that time making wills? I mean, a will is something my dad has!

A: Making a will forces us to think about our own mortality— and it can make us feel old. Keep in mind, though, that even if you live to a very old age, the patterns you establish early on in your marriage pave the way for how you conduct your future financial and legal affairs. And unfortunately young people die all the time. A will ensures that your assets—money, possessions, and property—are passed to the people you want to have them. Without a will, your state's laws dictate who receives what. With a will, you're in control. What's more, people who die intestate (without a will) often cause greater suffering for those they leave behind. Family conflict and even schisms result from the lack of clarity of your wishes: Your survivors might fight over who gets what. Think of making a will as an act of kindness toward your family.

Q: Let's say I make a will. I don't want the world knowing about my personal business, especially while I'm still alive. Are a lot of people going to know about its contents?

A: The only people who have to know the content of your will are the attorney who helps you draft the document and your spouse, whom you should consult anyway.

Q: All this stuff about insurance, wills, and saving money sounds very expensive. All those lawyers and accountants and policies—not to mention those annoying insurance salespeople! How much is this going to run me?

A: You can pay now and be in control of your life, or you can pay later according to the whim of the courts. Insurance, wills, and so on are actually investments. A few dollars smartly spent now will prevent financial disaster later on when the two of you—or, as the case may be, just one of you—are at your most vulnerable. In the scope of a lifetime, the expense is minimal. Also check with your employer, who may be able to offer some of these services (particularly life insurance) as part of your benefits package. Also, unions and professional organizations frequently offer insurance at a discount.

Q: How am I supposed to find the time to make a will?

A: It doesn't have to take a lot of time to draft a will. Be sure to hire an attorney who is sensitive to your time constraints. To be honest, people often spend more time waffling about whether to draft a will than they do on the will-creation process.

Q: My wife and I have a young son. If we die, I'm sure that some-one in my family will take over and care for him. This will spare me the expense of a lawyer, won't it?

A: If you die intestate, the courts and the state you live in will decide where your assets go (and the state will take some while it's at it) as well as who will take care of your children.

Q: Drafting a will is too complicated, isn't it?

A: It will be far more complicated for everyone—including your surviving spouse and children, if you have any—if you don't seize this opportunity to make some important decisions. Remember, take advantage of your good health to make clear to the world what you want done in the event of your death.

Q: How do I get started?

A: Start immediately! Don't delay. Stop thinking and start act-ing. Your family's future depends on both of you! Don't forget the im-portance of acting as a team. Any decisions you make about the future should be made together. These decisions can be monumental, so it's important that you share the responsibility.

Once you've decided to put your house in order, find a good attor-ney. Let word-of-mouth and referrals from reliable sources help you find an attorney. And remember, you don't need to retain an attorney permanently. Consulting a capable lawyer can set your mind at ease and help you accomplish your goals efficiently. It's also the best way to be sure your wills and other legal documents follow the letter of the law.

Interview several attorneys before you choose one. Select an attorney with an impeccable reputation. Ask yourself some questions too. Do you feel comfortable with the attorney? Consider the worst-case scenario: Can you envision her trekking down to the local courthouse to bail you out? Does he actively engage you in discussions about your concerns? Does she seem to understand your needs? Is he up-front with you about his fees? Does she feel comfortable with the kind of work you're asking her do to? Would he seek consultation with another attorney if he felt unfamiliar with some aspect of the law?

You don't need to be particularly well-organized to draw up a simple will. Basic wills (both you and your spouse should have one) are not expensive to draft. On the advice of your attorney, you'll both be asked to identify executors for your estates. The executor will help the lawyer settle the estate ethically and efficiently. An executor can be a family member, trusted friend, or attorney.

If you are wealthy, or plan to be, it's also crucial to find a good accountant. When choosing an accountant, use the same criteria you would for choosing an attorney.

> ❋ Rent a small safety-deposit box to store important documents in. Or consider buying a small fireproof safe or lockbox to keep in your home.

Q: What should we do to get organized for our meeting with the attorney?

A: One of the first things you need to do together is create a list of assets. If you and your spouse die, your family members, lawyer, and accountant will need to take inventory of your assets to settle your estate. Create a list of account numbers, insurance policies, investments, and all other assets and property. Provide copies to trusted family members, friends, and your attorney or accountant. Don't assume you have to be rich to create this list: It will grow as the two of you grow together. Update it regularly, about once a year.

> Consider videotaping or photographing the inside of your home to catalog all your possessions. Keep the tape or photos in a safety-deposit box or give copies to your attorney for safe keeping.

Q: What's the best way to approach life insurance?

A: Life insurance should do only one thing: pay your surviving spouse, children, and/or family members cash when you die. Insurance should provide your surviving family with enough money to live on, pay for the necessities of life, and educate your children, if necessary. Should you have life insurance? If either of you is dependent on the other for income, the answer is probably yes. If both spouses could get by without the other's income, then you probably do not need to buy life insurance at this time. Once a baby enters the picture, the equation changes. Purchasing high-quality term life insurance is a great way to protect your spouse and children should something happen to you.

Term life insurance is straightforward and reasonably priced. If you die, the insurance company pays your benefactors. This is pure insurance with no bells, whistles, or savings plans. You should purchase enough renewable term insurance to provide your loved ones with the lifestyle they're accustomed to. This amount generally equals at least six times your current yearly income. Choose a conservative major insurance company that has received high ratings from reliable sources.

Some couples choose to buy different forms of life insurance. Many of these policies are designed to double as insurance and a savings plan. They are more expensive and, since there are better ways to save, less desirable.

Should the nonworking parent of a child buy life insurance? Even if one parent doesn't earn an income, it's not a bad idea. If the nonworking spouse dies, his or her smaller policy can help pay for child care.

Should you buy life insurance for your child? Do you depend on your child for income? If the answer is no—and it probably is, unless you're being supported by your millionaire child-actor—don't bother:

"My dad told me to protect our savings, what little we have, by buying disability insurance. Is this a good idea?"

What if you get hurt at work? Or fall off your roof installing a satellite dish? Think about what would happen if you became severely injured or impaired. What if you're involved in an accident or require surgery? You can't work if you're severely injured or recovering from a bad accident. How will your family survive, especially if you have a child or a nonworking spouse? Who will pay the rent or mortgage? Disability insurance is expensive, but well worth it. If necessary, disability insurance will pay you a percentage of your income before you were injured. Each working spouse should have it. Some employers offer disability insurance as an employment benefit. Your policy should:

- *Be noncancelable*
- *Cover you until age 65*
- *Have a long waiting period to avoid high costs*
- *Waive the premium if you become disabled*

These are just the basics. For more information, read about disability insurance at your local library.

Q: What else can we do to be "responsible"?

A: Purchase health insurance. It would be a shame—and devastating—to have to spend your hard-earned savings if you or a family member becomes seriously ill or injured. If health care is not available through your or your spouse's employers, consider joining a health maintenance organization and paying for it yourselves.

Q: We have a child. What do I need to do to ensure that she won't be raised by weird Uncle Jim?

A: Name a guardian. The selection of someone to take care of your child in the event of your death is crucial. If you don't have wills, a court will appoint the guardian. Prospective guardians should share your values and be suited, physically and otherwise, to raise your child. A guardian can be a family member or trusted friend. Be sure to discuss the issue with your chosen guardian(s) before naming them in your wills. Remember that naming a guardian for your children is one of the ultimate expressions of love and concern for your family.

Q: What is a durable power of attorney?

A: It is a document allowing your husband, wife, or one of your parents, for example, to make legal, financial, or business decisions for you if you become injured or disabled and consequently unable to make competent choices for yourself. Everyone should have a durable power of attorney.

Q: *What is a living will?*

A: A living will is a nonbinding but nonetheless important health-care document. This "will" lets those who care for you—family, friends, and doctors—know your wishes in the event that you are unable to express them. A living will, which you should create now, specifies how you would like your family and doctors to make medical treatment decisions for you when you cannot make them yourself. Valid in most states, a living will makes clear, for example, whether or not you would wish to be kept on life support or have it removed in the event that you become comatose.

Your Life Together

Add the information in this chapter to your growing practical knowledge and take steps now to ensure that future generations are well cared for and at least have options. Planning for the future together shows how much you love each other, your family, and your children, if you have any. It would be wonderful if your life together could span a hundred years! If, by chance, it doesn't at least you'll know you took responsible and conscientious measures to provide for the well-being of your children and the surviving spouse. In the next chapter, we'll switch gears and take a look at another potentially unpleasant but common and usually short-lived event: kissing and making up.

· 6 ·

Kissing and Making Up

HOW TO SURVIVE YOUR FIRST
LOVERS' QUARREL

6

Whether you've been married one week or closer to one year, your first fight will come and go with varying degrees of pain and misery. If you're like most couples, you've probably had minor arguments while dating. Your love for one another will almost always override any temporary bad feelings that pass between you. But it sure feels terrible!

"'That's it,' I thought to myself. 'We're history.'"

There's nothing quite like your first post-wedding blowout. Why is your first fight as a married couple so significant and memorable? Probably because it will jolt you both into the reality that marriage is not all fun and games. For most married couples, the first fight signifies an end to the idealized splendor that was the proposal, wedding, honeymoon, and periods of settling in—positive experiences that characterized the first phase of your lives together.

Like everything else you do together, the way you approach and resolve disagreements will influence the way you treat each other for the rest of your lives. In this chapter, we'll look at what happens between newlyweds to cause fights, how to resolve the differences, and how to prevent them from recurring.

What's New with the Two of You?

Starting fights, getting pulled into them, experiencing them, and surviving them can all elicit a variety of feelings, thoughts, and behaviors. Sometimes identifying the feelings that accompany conflict can be enormously helpful during the resolution phase. Here are some common feelings that may arise as a result of your first fight.

YOU MAY BE FEELING . . .

Panic, Dread, and Anxiety   How could you not? You've invested time, money, and tremendous emotional energy into the relationship. To have it seemingly crumble to pieces before your eyes can feel like a disaster:

> *"I remember our first fight. I was hysterical. I thought it was over. After all we'd been through together! I was fantasizing about how to break it to my family that we were finished. I panicked and didn't know what to do. A sense of doom overtook me. Although it would only be the first in a lifetime of arguments together, on that day it just seemed so darned final."*

Your first fight feels like it lasts an eternity, but chances are if you and your wife or husband look back on it ten years later, neither of you will be able to recover the details.

Anger   Regardless of the subject matter and despite any objective anger that arises, couples may feel angry at the fight itself. Your courtship probably wasn't flawless, but some people still cling to the notion of perfection in marriage and reject the idea that marriage is hard work. Those who share an idyllic view of marriage may be caught by surprise, which can make them angry:

> *"I thought marriage was supposed to be love, love, love. All I'm feeling now is anger, aggravation, and pain. Who wrote the book of love anyway? Edgar Allan Poe?"*

> ✥ Remind yourselves that the first fight most often symbolizes nothing more than two people trying to feel their way around each other's emotional space.

You shouldn't lower your expectations altogether, but it might help to remember that you're both very different in some ways. Rather than reacting against your differences, try to rejoice in them. As we'll see later, some of the best learning experiences come from disruption of marital harmony.

Fear   There are many different kinds of fear associated with fighting and arguments. One common type is an overwhelming fear of the potential loss of your spouse:

> *"We recently had an argument, our first big one. My wife packed her things and left for her mother's house. It scared the heck out of me. I felt so vulnerable and alone. It was really frightening."*

In most cases, the fear, vulnerability, and tenuous feelings associated with these temporary separations are, thankfully, short-lived. But they clearly remind us how hard we have to work to grow together.

Uncertainty Life, like picking the fastest-moving line at the Department of Motor Vehicles, is full of uncertainty. A big argument about something important to you both can fill you with a confusing sense of crystal-clear uncertainty:

> *"I've never seen my husband react the way he did to me during that heated 'discussion.' I have absolutely no idea what to do."*

There are many different forms of uncertainty. Many couples feel unsure of how to approach an argument, how to resolve it, how to deal with its after-effects, or how to avoid the problem the next time.

Relief Are disagreements always bad for you? Not at all. Many couples, once they weather their first downpour of conflict, feel thankful it's over:

> *"In a nutshell, we got married, fought, talked, made up, and went on our merry ways together. Perfection in an imperfect world! What a relief."*

> *"We broke the ice and had our first major problem. Wasn't so bad. I think we came out of it stronger. Now I guess we can make it through anything."*

Sadness Nobody likes fighting. Having fights, depending on the subject matter and outcome, can certainly lead to or trigger dysphoria, or great sadness. Some couples even perceive a fight as a loss in itself. The first fight represents the loss of the blissful innocence that may have initially characterized your relationship. The entry into a different phase of your lives together can be jolting:

> *"I know that ever since we had our first big disagreement things just haven't been the same. It's almost as if we both suffered some kind of shock or something."*

Impulsiveness   Fights have a way of prodding us to say and do things we might not ordinarily say or do—and often regret later on. Trying to win an argument, sometimes at any expense, often leads to disinhibition—the consequences of which may be felt for a long time:

> *"The first time we got into an argument, we both kind of went nuts. I screamed and yelled, she slammed doors. I ended up leaving for a day or two. We said some things that night that we'll always regret. Over what? Stupid stuff."*

Remember your childhood lessons— think before you speak.

Frustration and Resentment   Who wouldn't feel resentful after a huge blowout? After all, you were both trying to champion your respective causes—and nobody seemed to be listening. There's nothing worse than feeling as though you're not being heard or understood.

Disappointment   You may feel let down by your relationship and your temporary inability to resolve important issues in your marriage. This happens to almost everybody at some point, or points, along the journey together. Don't worry. In most cases, such feelings are short-lived.

Remorse   As we've seen, people say things in the heat of battle that they don't really mean. Try to keep things in perspective. You'll feel different about things once you've had a chance to cool down.

Despite the hurt feelings and pain caused by your first major fight, keep in mind that these effects are temporary. But if you're still worried about the long-term repercussions of your first fight, just ask any experienced married couple what their first big argument was about. Chances are, they won't remember.

Overcoming Your New Obstacles

You've survived your first fight. What was it all about? How did it start? What are the common themes? If you haven't had your first fight yet, congratulations. But can you predict what you will fight about? Something good? Something worth fighting over? Perhaps you imagine that you'll fight about how to get closer to God, how much money to give to charity, how often to invite complete strangers into your home for a meal.

Sorry to disappoint you, but your first blowout will very likely not make your religious adviser proud. More often than not, newlyweds fight about things that, at the time, seem much more important than they really are. Be prepared to abandon your idealized image of principled debate and get ready to address ultimately trivial questions such as "Who left the water on?" "Why did you burn the toast?" "Where did all the money go?" "Why can't you keep your toenails shorter?" "Why are *your* socks in *my* drawer?" and the ultimately unanswerable "Who do you think you are anyway?"

Despite the fact that most arguments are petty, the reality is that they seem, at the time, far more significant. It can be tough for two different personalities to feel their way around each other for the first time—and for the rest of your lives! Here are some subjective issues that can be precursors to big fights.

SUBJECTIVE PRECURSORS TO FIGHTS

Character Differences Sometimes the differences between us can lead to conflict. Our personalities are usually fairly fixed by the time we're in our twenties. As a result, we each perceive the world and our surroundings differently.

Unresolved Family Issues   As we've seen, external pressures can often influence the way we respond to one another.

Inflexibility and Self-Centeredness   All married couples can sometimes get caught up in the routine of living together. This can sometimes lead to a lack of flexibility, and selfishness.

Understimulation   Boredom can often lead to dissatisfaction and fights.

Stress of Responsibility   Issues related to personal responsibility—taking care of the apartment or house, earning a living, and doing the household chores—can very easily spark an argument.

Leading Separate Lives   Sometimes, before the two of you know it, you'll have emotionally or symbolically moved into different rooms of the apartment.

Ignoring Each Other's Emotional Needs   It's very easy to remember your own feelings. It's less comfortable and convenient to have to keep track of your partner's.

Taking Each Other for Granted   While classically developing after several years of marriage, if you've been together for years or lived together prior to your marriage, don't be too surprised if this isn't at the root of some of your recent issues. It's easy to consider *your* needs and to rely on your spouse's unconditional love and attention, even if you're not emotionally present all of the time.

Lack of Feeling   When you and your mate stop feeling for each other, you're bound to run into trouble sooner or later.

Poor Communication Fights and arguments typically start and end with disrupted communication. Failing to engage with your spouse quickly, at the first sign of trouble, will usually lead to a bigger problem.

There are many other precursors to fights, but these are some of the most common types. Now let's examine the common types of fights that arise from these precursors.

COMMON FIGHT THEMES

Money As we've seen, money has a way of squeezing itself between you and your husband or wife. What are the problems? You name it. Joint accounts, separate accounts, jealousy, making too little, spending too much, not saving, living beyond your means, poor spending habits, bad budgeting, being too frugal or downright cheap, spending your spouse's inheritance, borrowing money, credit card debt, forgetting to pay taxes, not paying bills, not consulting with your spouse before making a major purchase. The list goes on and on.

Relatives Like the list for potential money problems, the list for relatives goes on and on. You hate them, she loves them, she hates them, you're ambivalent about them, they visit too much, they stay too long, they're inconsiderate, they insult you, you insult them.

Inconsiderate Behavior This list goes on as well. Most fights can be traced to these problems:

> *"I sent my husband to buy milk. He stopped at a bar on his way home and came back hours later. No milk."*

> *"Our first big fight dealt with the serious subject of who'd get which side of the bed."*

This list includes household chores, dirty socks, underwear in the hamper, laundry, after-dinner cleanup, and cooking. But it can also include not giving up time for the other person, going out with old friends, staying out late, being selfish, acting jealous, not sharing responsibilities, and seeing old flames.

Sex   One or the other of you may feel you have too much or too little, or that the other person is selfish in bed.

Job   One spouse works, but she travels too much. One spouse doesn't work, or he earns less than the other and spends all his wife's money.

Serious Problems   In the worst case, serious issues like substance abuse, abusive behavior, and perceived or real infidelity can be a source of friction.

In the next few sections, we'll explore the benefits of fighting fair as well as several ways you can resolve issues and prevent conflict from escalating.

It Just Keeps Getting Better

Why is it important to learn to contain conflict and resolve it reasonably? There's an enormous variety of things to fight over. Why? People come up with all sorts of things—all of which are important to them—to disagree over. It's human nature to disagree. And there's nothing

> Remember to meet in neutral territory. Go somewhere you both feel comfortable.

How to Fight Fair and Resolve Conflict Calmly

Conflict resolution should really be a two-pronged effort: prevention and problem solving. Get used to talking to each other. Every now and then take the time to ask each other a few of these preventive questions. Once the two of you have established a dialogue, you'll find it much easier to resolve important issues.

1. *Become accustomed to talking with each other on a regular basis.*

It may help to ask each other some of the following questions:

- Can we do more for each other? Are we interested in helping each other through the tough times? Can we work together to find common ground?
- Have we considered each other's desires and needs? Are we able to express ourselves and our needs, and are we each receptive to hearing the needs of the other?
- Are you aware of how stressful my day is? Do you know what I do at work? How is my work-induced stress affecting our lives together?

wrong with that. The danger lies in repeated, unresolved arguments, which can lead to resentment, communication problems, a stressful marriage, and possibly, divorce. How do you prevent that? Attend to the basics.

While there will undoubtedly be many combinations of issues that develop as the two of you grow together, the ways in which you resolve them now, during the initial stages of your lives together, will form a template for future conflict resolution. What are the advantages of fighting fair and resolving arguments?

- Now that we're married, what's the emotional value of our lives together? Is it different than before?
- What impact does the marriage have on our daily routines? Are things different? If so, how? What caused the change?
- How are we communicating with each other? Do we talk with each other enough?
- Are we taking each other for granted? How can we be better at listening to each other?
- Are there things I'm doing that really bother you?
- Do we take each other seriously?
- Do we take each other and ourselves *too* seriously?
- When was the last time we laughed together?
- What can we do to improve our relationship?

You and your partner should meet from time to time to discuss how your lives have been inexorably changed for the better as a result of your marriage. Do your best to facilitate communication with your husband or wife, try not to lose your collective sense of humor, and don't take yourselves too seriously. After all, you're both still learning and growing together.

(continued on next page)

Prevent Discord This is really the most important issue. You must determine a way to resolve your conflicts in a civilized fashion, prevent a permanent disruption in your life, save face, and learn from the experience so you can move on together.

Prevent Impulsiveness Effective conflict resolution will help prevent you from acting out in a way that is sure to damage your relationship. We'll take a closer look at this subject in Chapter 10.

KISSING AND MAKING UP

(Focus—continued)

2. Temporarily suspend your opinion of who's right and who's wrong.

One of the hardest things about fighting is the feeling that you're not being heard, listened to, or understood by your partner. Get used to stepping outside yourself for a minute or two and really listening to your spouse. It's much easier to agree to disagree when both of you understand each other's perspectives.

3. Contain your anger.

If you're the sort of person who angers quickly, try to remember that you may soon be setting an example for other, yet unborn, members of your family. Also, don't forget that intense rage and screaming is frightening—and won't build your partner's confidence in you. If necessary, give yourselves a cooling off period— a time-out. Take a five-minute break. That way, you more likely avoid name-calling, insults, and abusive language you'll regret later. Remember, there's no prize for who ends a fight first. Take your time.

4. Deal with panic and anxiety.

Don't let panic turn into impulsiveness. It's important to remember that feelings can be warning signs. They should not be

Create a Healthy Home Environment Chances are, you won't always be the only ones living in your home. There's no better reason to resolve fights fairly than to create a healthy, supportive environment where your children can flourish. Learning to resolve problems peacefully and effectively now, while your relationship is still

allowed to govern your every action, but don't ignore them either. Avoid acting out in anger or behaving destructively out of anxiety. Do not issue threats.

5. Do not take solace in alcohol or drugs.

Drinking before, during, or after an argument is ill-advised. Why? For one thing, the disinhibiting effects of alcohol can make matters worse. The use of alcohol and drugs can cause a variety of unpleasant, unhelpful, and often frightening behaviors.

6. Look for common ground and opportunities for compromise.

The importance of compromise can't be emphasized enough. Does this mean you need to sacrifice your principals? Hardly. But if the two of you search intensely, you're bound to take small, confidence-building steps that neither of you oppose.

7. Use the gifts of time and perspective.

It's true, time does tend to heal wounds. Take a step back every now and then, especially during a fight. Try to remember that you do not need to resolve the argument immediately. With the advantage of time and perspective, it will become far easier to see the problem from all angles and, as a result, solve it. Likewise, agree with your husband or wife to resolve major

(continued on next page)

young, will help prevent small ears from hearing and small eyes from seeing certain petty misadventures with each other later.

Create a Physically and Emotionally Healthy Climate

Fighting fair will help lower the overall stress level in your home. The

(Focus—continued)

differences last, or later. Cling to common ground, and while you're waiting to solve the problem, get on with your lives.

8. Sometimes the better person is the one who breaks the silence.

It's not easy. Sometime between the time you're married and the end of the first year, you'll more than likely have an argument followed by an episode of strained silence. You're not conceding anything by breaking the ice with a "Hey, we need to talk about this," or "Hey, your fly is undone" (humor can be a great ice-breaker). Breaking the silence will only strengthen your relationship and encourage the conflict resolution and closure.

9. If necessary, get help.

Some fights just snowball. If you find that your first "big fights" are repeating themselves over and over again—each one getting

result? Fewer physical and emotional problems as a couple and as a family.

Encourage Teamwork Anything the two of you do together constructively, whether it's traveling to new places or working together to resolve conflict, reinforces the concept of the team—something you can always fall back on.

As you both grow and learn how to live with one another, don't forget that issues and problems tend to develop gradually, rather than appearing spontaneously. How can you prevent the buildup of conflict and learn to resolve issues peacefully? Read the Focus section "Love and

worse and more intense—you probably need some help to re-solve the underlying issues. Don't get off on the wrong foot. Ask a trusted friend, doctor, or religious adviser to refer you to a good couples' therapist. Your sessions need not be lengthy, time-consuming, expensive, or even ongoing. Sometimes just having someone point out the differences in your personal styles is all it takes to get back on track.

10. Delight in your differences.

I've always liked the saying "Through chaos comes creativity." Very often, the differences between the two of you will drive you toward understanding and enjoyment of each other. Don't run away from the stress, strain, and chaos of your first fight. If you stick with it and fight fair, you'll end up learning more about each other. You'll also develop your own ways of dealing with the stresses of life together, as a team.

War" (page 128), to discover techniques you can use to help diffuse and discourage tension.

Being There for Each Other

What now? So far, you've argued and have undoubtedly experienced a multitude of feelings—some quite strong and unpleasant. What do you do now? Keep in mind that resolving differences takes time. It's a process that has to develop and mature. As you both learn to feel your way around each other, you'll soon discover the best ways to fix what's broken. The Focus section "How to Fight Fair and Resolve Conflict

> ### FOCUS
> ## *Love and War*
>
> Can't break the ice after your first fight? Here are some suggestions:
>
> - *Get out your tapes:* If you've been taping any of your "firsts"—first purchase as a married or engaged couple, first intimate chat during the honeymoon. and so on—invite your husband to sit with you and listen to your tapes. It will help the two of you put things back in perspective.
> - *Make up a playful invitation:* Invite your wife to a "conflict-resolution party." Make dinner, light candles, discuss the trouble.
> - *Take a leap of faith:* Break the ice by renting a movie you both love to watch together. Put it on and wait for your spouse to walk in. Ask him to watch it with you.
> - *Have a conflict-resolution party to celebrate the fact that it's all over:* Put the details of the first fight down on your "firsts" calendar. Then, get on with your lives.

Calmly" (page 122), provides some general guidelines for forming the basis of future conflict resolution.

Your Life Together

Who knew that your first argument could be so complicated? And what a pain in the neck! As you grow and learn more about each other, you'll undoubtedly develop your own styles of argument and conflict resolution. Talking openly and frequently with each other is the key to a successful marriage. If you're talking reasonably, you're not fighting. In the next chapter, we'll take a look at how to keep the flame of love and romance burning.

· 7 ·

Intimacy, Romance, and Sex

KEEPING THE FLAME LIT AFTER
THE HONEYMOON

7

Your first married year together is a great time to enjoy the warmth and love you've worked so hard to achieve together. Showing each other how in love you are will keep the flames of romance alive:

> *"This is the most carefree time of my life. Being with my new wife— expressing my love for her and enjoying her—is an unparalleled experience."*

What's New with the Two of You?

One of the core features of a solid marriage—no matter how many anniversaries you celebrate—is the physical, emotional, and spiritual closeness the two of you share. The advantages of love, sex, romance, and intimacy are numerous. You'll grow together, be happy, feel more satisfied with your lives, and seek each other out over the years for warmth, security, reassurance, and fun! While you have certainly shared

FOCUS

Reading the Warning Signs: A Checklist

- *Are you spending less time together?* Are your habits shifting for no apparent reason? Often, jobs and other legitimate responsibilities force changes in the amount of time and in the way the two of you spend time together. But you can typically compensate for necessary changes by making other adjustments in your schedules. Is this happening?
- *Are you making excuses for not being together?*
- *Would you rather be with friends, or anybody else besides your husband or wife?* This is a not-so-subtle sign. Are you planning to spend more time with anybody but your partner this week? Do you feel that your partner is avoiding you? Have others replaced you?
- *Would you rather be alone than together?* Are you coming home after work and cloistering yourself in the basement, the garage, or some other room? Is your spouse isolating himself or herself from you?

plenty of romance, most newly married couples continue to learn new things about themselves and each other as time passes. In fact, your intimacy "education" will be ongoing. Nurturing strong physical and emotional closeness will work wonders for you and your future family—and help keep you feeling young, healthy, and content. In this chapter, we'll take a look at what the two of you can do to maintain—and even improve—your love life.

- *Are you thinking romantically about other people with increasing frequency?* There's nothing wrong with sexual fantasy. But if it becomes consuming it's possible that your preoccupation prevents you from having a meaningful relationship with your marital partner. Does your husband or wife mention other people to you? Does he or she seem preoccupied with another person's looks?

- *Have you stopped being playful?* Chances are the two of you were playful with each other during your courtship. You probably didn't take things so seriously, shared good times together, and treated each other with greater patience and a sense of humor. Has any of that changed? Are things less fun than they used to be? Do you find that your collective sense of humor is diminished, or gone? Can you still tease each other playfully?

- *Do you argue more often?* As we saw in Chapter 6, you're sure to have an initial argument or two. Do you find that you're having more and more "first arguments" about nontrivial, fundamental issues? Are you irritating each other? If so, and

(continued on next page)

The Wonders of Intimacy

You got married for a variety of great reasons. Chances are, you had many common interests, got along well, and fell in love. You also undoubtedly learned enough about each other to feel intimately connected. The "connection" is the key. There are many different ways to

(Focus—continued)

    if the bad feelings are not resolved, it could mean that something is amiss.

- *Are either of you increasingly bored with the other?* Do you fall asleep in your macaroni and cheese when your husband talks to you about his day? Are you finding that your wife has an increasingly shorter attention span for your riveting tales?
- *Have you started to abandon your joint traditions?* The slow erosion of traditions—things the two of you have established together as special activities, days, or rituals, like going to the movies on a certain day, cooking for each other, and back rubs—can signal a deterioration in your feelings for each other.
- *Has your sex life changed for the worse?* Are the two of you making love less often than usual for no apparent reason? Aside from exhaustion, out-of-town job responsibilities, or other legitimate reasons, have you noticed an overall change in the quality or quantity of sex? Do you share affectionate statements or physical expressions of affection less often?
- *Do you enjoy each other's company?* You probably assume that you would notice if you were *not* enjoying each other. But often the shift is subtle and happens before you know it.

connect with one another—sexually, emotionally, socially, and so on. All these connections are different forms of intimacy. Sometimes intimacy is as simple as talking softly about life together or spending special time together. You should strive together to develop many forms of intimacy.

    Why work on building intimacy? Remember that setting the tone during the first year will help foster even greater love and admiration

- *Have you been more concerned with your own feelings than those of your partner?* When combined with many of the other signs in this list, this is a sure sign that something is amiss.
- *Is your mate flirting excessively with other people?* Most of the time, casual flirting doesn't mean anything. Flirtatious behavior seems to be a part of some people's character. But when it occurs with increasing frequency or intensity, or, if it develops from nowhere, it's time to start questioning the health of your marriage.
- *Are you feeling guilty about your behavior or thoughts?* Guilty feelings can be extremely oppressive. For example, if after reading this list you start to feel a little guilty about your behavior, it's time to do something. Later in the chapter, we'll discuss how you can get your marriage back on track.
- *Have you started to use drugs or drink heavily?* This is a certain sign that there are problems with some aspect of your life.

If you're able to look at your behavior in the context of the questions on this list, it probably means that you've started the process to repair what's broken. After all, the two of you got married for all the right reasons. It may be time to get back to the basics—review what made your relationship great in the first place.

for each other as you grow together. Capturing and caring for that special closeness you had during courtship is essential. Being intimate with each other pulls the two of you closer together and farther away from the trials and tribulations of the day. You'll also learn to be more receptive and responsive to cues from your spouse. You'll feel special, honored, and blessed. There will be times in your lives—having children, for example—when relaxing together comes at a premium! Being

---

FOCUS

Keep the Flame Burning

- *Establish an early warning system.* Refer periodically to the checklist of warning signs on page 132. From time to time, go through the list and ask yourselves all of the questions.
- *Meet regularly to discuss your emotional bankbook.* You discuss money with some regularity, right? Sometimes you need to balance your emotional checkbook too. Using the checklist again, take your emotional pulse.
- *Strive to create an ambiance of romance from dusk to dawn.* Is it realistic to think that you can maintain the level of romantic intensity all of the time? Probably not. But it's certainly fun to try!
- *Make small gestures count in a big way.* A series of small niceties adds up quickly. And doing nice things for each other will reinforce feelings of respect, love, and admiration. Take time off from work to be together, but instead of using all your vacation time at once, consider taking a series of long weekends. Use the time to go away together—or just stay

---

"good" at it now will help save time and energy later on. What else? It's fun to be that close—in so many ways—to another person! Still not convinced? Read on.

YOU MAY BE FEELING

Romantic   One type of intimacy is romance! The two of you may be deeply in love and romancing each other to embarrassing proportions. Being in love and making love are wonderful gifts:

home. Establish a "date night"—a night during the week that
you'll always spend together, no matter how you're feeling
about each other at the time. Be creative.

- *Use the time-tested gifts of patience, compromise, respect, and
humor to resolve issues.* Accept no substitute. These ingredi-
ents should form the cornerstone of your relationship. The
best way to keep the flame alive is to always strive to achieve
these ideals.

- *Maintain the emotional integrity of the team.* If you're doing
your emotional accounting and reviewing important questions with yourself and each other periodically, you'll have
a far better chance of keeping your team together.

- *Don't worry alone.* Are there some things you can't discuss
with your partner? Seeking out therapy or counseling, rather
than bearing the burden alone, can be extremely liberating.
Sometimes simply discussing it in the open with a trained
counselor can help reduce anxiety.

- *Maintain the proper perspective.* Remind yourself why you got
married in the first place. Couples often lose sight of the

(continued on next page)

*"I seem to be incapable of not touching this woman [my wife]
in a romantic way. She makes me crazy, nuts, aroused and all
sorts of other private words. I love it. We're by far the friskiest
couple around."*

Content and Secure   Being intimate with your spouse is reassuring—especially after a long day at work. The pressures of the day melt
away, replaced by feelings of security and happiness:

(Focus—continued)

reasons for their initial attraction to each other. Don't let this happen to you.

- *Don't be impulsive.* If you're thinking of negatively acting out a feeling or thought, you'll almost always regret rushing into it impulsively. It's a good idea to decide on important issues slowly, after a lot of thought. Seek counseling if you're unable to openly discuss these problems with your spouse. When in doubt, wait it out.
- *Don't be afraid to ask questions.* Ask yourselves what's happening in your marriage that might be contributing to your unhappiness. Give yourselves the opportunity to review individual issues with a competent therapist first.
- *Subliminate.* Use sublimation, a defense mechanism, to avoid acting on your impulses. That is, channel your urges into activities that are more socially acceptable. Join a gym, develop hobbies, read a book, write a book, co-write a book, talk with trusted friends, take time for yourself, or use fantasy.

"Sometimes when we get home from a tough day at work, we cuddle up together on the couch and just talk about the day. Just the two of us, together, sharing time. It's special and unique."

Appreciated and Loved   Feeling appreciated by your spouse really goes a long way:

"He makes me feel as special today as he did four years ago when we first met. His attitude is that our lives should feel like one long date. One terrific first kiss that's lasting forever."

Close   The special bond between man and woman will never be stronger than when the two of you share private moments.

Focused Feelings of intimacy foster a special concentration or focus. The rest of the world tends not to matter as much, at least for a while, once you've established a sense of intimacy, warmth, and closeness.

Sometimes, despite your best efforts, romance, love, sex, and intimacy take a back seat to other seemingly more pressing issues:

"We've both been so terrible busy. Who has time?"

Some married couples' feelings about their lives together change. Is this always a bad thing? Not at all. As people learn to grow together, feelings and thoughts about each other may change—most often for the better. Sometimes, the intensity of romance and intimacy can temporarily fade. Sounds serious! But it doesn't need to be. Most married couples will experience fluctuations in their feelings for each other. See the Focus section "Keep the Flame Burning" (page 136), for ways to avoid this before it happens.

Feeling stressed and alone? Seek out trusted, experienced married friends. You shouldn't be embarrassed to ask for advice from older couples, who have probably weathered similar storms in the past.

Taken to the extremes, couples in trouble may end up feeling a variety of very unpleasant feelings: ignored or neglected, unloved, taken for granted, betrayed, bored with each other, and so on. But for the

FOCUS

Romance Update: Quick Tips

How can you get back on the romantic track? Consider the following ideas:

- *Take the time to write down five reasons you married your spouse.* Share those reasons with each other and see what happens.
- *Periodically review your book of "firsts" together.* You'll be surprised how quickly loving memories return.
- *Every time you hear "your song" on the radio, agree to go out together sometime during the week to talk about your lives together.*
- *Change your routine to prevent boredom and develop empathy.* If you don't usually make dinner, try making it one night. Do the shopping or laundry. Sleep on the other side of the bed one night. Switch chores.
- *Continue to build on the momentum you developed during courtship—don't take shortcuts.*

most part, while some of these thoughts, feelings, and behaviors sound terribly disheartening, they can also be helpful, serving as early warning signs that something is amiss. Don't forget that most married couples will experience at least a few of these uncomfortable feelings at some point in the marriage. If the two of you can recognize the potential problems early on and resolve them, you'll strengthen your relationship phenomenally.

- *Be creative and thoughtful.*
- *Learn to be a bit self-sacrificing for your spouse.*
- *Be open to new romantic ideas.* If it feels funny or if you're embarrassed, start slowly. Communicate your feelings to each other.
- *Compliment each other for a great sexual or romantic encounter.*
- *Gently tell your mate what you like or don't like about his or her sexual technique.*
- *Erotic pictures can spice things up a bit.* Experiment.
- *Surf the Internet together for erotic pictures.*
- *Don't underestimate the power of language.* Talk to each other during lovemaking.
- *Make Valentine's Day a once-a-month affair.*
- *Join the Secret-of-the-Month Club.* Tell each other a secret about yourself each month that no one else—up to this point—knows.
- *Send or write provocative, sexy notes to each other.* Leave them in interesting places around the house.
- *Accept sexual fantasy as normal and exciting.*

(continued on next page)

Overcoming Your New Obstacles

We all fall into routines—an increase in job pressure, a decrease in sex and romance, for example. In fact, depending on what's causing stress in the relationship, we all episodically and temporarily lose loving, romantic feelings for each other. What might you notice? How

(Focus—continued)

- *Pretend that your next sexual encounter with each other is your first ever.*
- *Enhance your sex lives by using a variety of different techniques.*
- *Try role playing.*
- *You don't need to share all your thoughts and fantasies with each other.* Sometimes taking time to become familiar with your own body and your own feelings will help the overall health of the relationship.
- *Stay in good health—emotional and physical.* Be sure to care for and about yourself.
- *Be playful, even juvenile, with each other.*
- *Be spontaneous.*
- *Play hooky from work.* Seduce and lure your spouse into bed (or the bathtub or other romantic spot). Stay there the whole day.
- *Initiate sex when both of you would be least likely to do it.*
- *Send your spouse a package with sexy underwear in it.*
- *Close all the blinds and spend the evening walking around the house naked.*
- *Send a provocative e-mail message or telegram to your spouse at work.*
- *Leave a nice, sexy message on his/her voice mail.*

can you tell? Take a look at the Focus section "Reading the Warning Signs: A Checklist" (page 132); then we'll look at some fun and easy ideas to get you back on track in the Focus section "Romance Update: Quick Tips" (page 140).

- *Write a sexy, suggestive short story with yourselves as the main characters.*
- *Send your spouse a voucher for one night out on the town with you.*
- *Eat dinner in the nude (at home).*
- *Constantly relive and recapture your first date, kiss, or intimate moment together.*
- *Talk about your first date regularly.*
- *Pretend you're going out together for the first time.*
- *Deal with sexual differences (how often, who initiates, and so on) through dialogue and compromise.*
- *Don't confuse the physical act of sex with love, admiration, respect, or intimacy.*
- *Spend an entire evening together doing just what he wants.*
- *Spend the next night together doing just what she wants.*
- *Kiss each other frequently.*
- *Hold hands.*
- *Refer to your spouse as "my love" as often as possible.*
- *Whenever you sit down next to your wife, rub her neck.*
- *Learn the names of all his relatives and ask him how Uncle Frank is doing every once in a while.*

(continued on next page)

It Just Keeps Getting Better

There's really nothing more important than working together to continue your loving journey together. What a great time this is! The first

> *(Focus—continued)*
> - *Ask her to tell you about pieces of her childhood—family trips, pets, schoolmates, and so on.*
> - *Learn all the details of his family and make a family tree for him, with commentary.*
> - *Secretly invite her best friend over for a weekend and send them out on a mini shopping spree together.*
> - *Take a trip to Niagara Falls, or another romantic resort, and rent a room with a round bed.*
> - *Give a back rub without asking for one in return.*

year of marriage should be a fantastically romantic and sexy time. A time of shared intimacy, quiet dinners together making plans, discussing the future, and learning even more about giving and sharing your love. What's the key to developing, maintaining, or even improving your time together? Are there still some things the two of you can learn about yourselves and each other? What can you do together to enhance your love lives? Again, the Focus section on page 140 will help you out.

Your Life Together

As one of the many spokes in the wheel of a solid marriage, intimacy should remain strong throughout your lives together. Keeping the flame alive is just one of the fun responsibilities and pleasures you'll encounter. Try to remember that feeling close to a special person will provide each of you with a wonderful future together. Work hard to please yourselves and each other. You can't go wrong.

· 8 ·

Being Social

OUT AND ABOUT AS A COUPLE

8

As the two of you make your way through the wonders of your first year together, remember that one of the reasons you're together is to have fun:

"Our social lives actually got better after we got married."

You've probably gotten pretty good at enjoying each other's company and have managed to spend considerable time getting to know each other better:

"In some ways, we're over the 'getting to know each other' stage. What I really want is for us to have a very active social life."

There are so many new issues to face. How important is an active social life? Can it really make a difference? Are you meeting other newlywed couples? What if you've moved away to a different part of the country—away from your friends and families? Have you been able to hook up with new friends? What about your friends who are still single? They will have to deal with their "loss" of a single friend and your gain. What's preventing you from having more social contact? In this chapter, we'll explore your new social lives together. While some of it might be the same as usual, being married opens up new social possibilities.

What's New with the Two of You?

If you're like many newly married couples, you may be caught between wanting to maintain intimacy with your partner and getting out to meet the world as a couple:

> *"Sometimes we prefer to just stay at home. We've actually had to push ourselves to get out and meet new people."*

Given the tremendous pressures and joys associated with the wedding and everything else the two of you have accomplished together, it seems natural to want to take a break from being in public. Sooner or later though, you'll want to get out again. Establishing patterns early on makes it that much simpler to maintain a comfortable lifestyle as you grow older together. How complicated can that be? Well, for many couples, it's not complicated at all. For others, it's a little trickier:

> *"I'd really like to meet more people. You know, do the 'adult' thing. But my husband, bless his soul, he's beat after work and all he wants to do is watch TV. It doesn't seem fair."*

Despite your differences, there's plenty of room for both of you to get what you want. Here are some important things to consider.

YOU MAY BE FEELING . . .

Excited and Blissfully Content
What's there to be excited about? Plenty:

"I know it sounds silly, but when I saw my credit card with my new last name on it, I got really excited. I had always written out what my new last name would be, but seeing it out there was really something else."

For some couples, their marriage offers a new social beginning:

"I was always the shy type. I'm not saying I hide behind my wife, but it's just so much easier to meet people now that we're always together. She's very gregarious and I'm—well, I've been compared to tree bark. But she helps me climb out of my shell."

For other couples, remembering childhood social activities gives them a warm feeling about their marriage and its social potential:

"My parents, unlike my wife's folks, always had people over for big, fancy parties to play cards or just to have a drink once in a while. Being married really makes me think about their past, and all the fun they had. Now I can have that fun too."

Alienated   Being married opens up new social horizons for some, but others complain of feeling cut off:

"Since we got married, I haven't been able to see my old single friends or do the social things I want to do. I feel totally isolated from the rest of humanity."

You may also be feeling a different sort of alienation:

"Whenever my husband's old friends come over, they always yuck it up together and try their hardest to exclude me. My husband tells me it's his time and that I should grow up. The truth is that I don't have my friends over on purpose, so that I can spend my free time with him. He doesn't seem to appreciate it."

Of course it's important to spend time together, but you must also realize that, unless one of you is using company as an excuse not to be with the other, being with old friends is acceptable, even desirable.

There's a different sort of loneliness that accompanies isolation:

"We've moved and, to be perfectly honest, I hate it here. I'm surprised we have running water. But that's not really the half of it. I have no friends or family here. My husband works and I'm just starting to look for work. I feel extremely lonely and isolated."

Moving can be a major trauma, especially if you've lived in one place for many years. Moving to another area or an entirely different part of the country can be painful and disruptive. Later in the chapter we'll take a look at ways to meet new people, wherever you may find yourself.

Anxious Does it sometimes feel like everyone else has friends but you?

"I feel sort of envious of people whose lives seem more settled. They always seem to be having people over or are frequently invited out. And here we sit."

Jealousy can arise from other circumstances too:

"My wife has tons of friends. I have very few. In fact, most of my friends are her friends. I don't know how she does it. I'm thankful I have some companionship, but I feel like I need some of my own friends."

Sometimes, people seem to fall into a routine and don't naturally seek out other people to be with. Lots of times, your personality may not lend itself to meeting and becoming friends with new people that easily.

Bored and Depressed Boredom and loneliness seem to go together:

"All I do is sit here all day and read the local tabloids. What a life."

You don't need to hit the town every night, singing and dancing on tables, but a decreased or nonexistent social life leads to dissatisfaction, dismay, and depression. It can adversely affect your marriage:

Conflicted About Time and Space Issues No, I'm not talking about the fourth dimension:

> *"I'm confused about time issues. I mean, I've always liked to do things on my own while my husband has always been more interested in doing things together. I can't stand him anymore—in an affectionate way, of course. I really need more time and space to do the things I want to do. I'm suffocating."*

> *"My wife is very independent. I admit it, I'm needier than she is. I like to be with her as much as possible. She thinks I'm a pest. We're running into a bit of trouble with each other in that sense. You know, issues of space. How do we sort it out?"*

You don't always have to be together. It's important to continue making time for individual pursuits. We'll look at these time and space issues in greater detail later in the chapter.

Confused What are the most serious feelings associated with the change marriage brings to your social lives? Couples often complain about not seeing eye-to-eye on any number of topics:

> *"I'm upset. I can't go out with my friends, I can't watch the football game, I can't have a beer. I can't do anything. Since we got married, she's been into this 'responsibility' thing. I don't get it. I want things to be the way they've always been."*

Despite any misgivings you might have about your social lives together, being social with each other and with peers is a healthy way to express yourselves. Having fun, in addition to your other responsibilities, will go a long way toward ensuring a healthy and happy marriage.

The goal is to start off on the right foot so that the rest of your lives together are as harmonious as they can be.

Overcoming Your New Obstacles

Why is there conflict in marriage? Is it because couples don't agree on every single issue? No. Within a marriage, there's plenty of room for varying degrees of discord. Do marriages fail because two people who are so different can't live together? Hardly. People do it, successfully, all the time. There's nothing wrong with being different.

What about similarities? Do people who are too similar get into trouble? Not usually. Conflict often arises because husbands and wives tend to drift too far away from each other emotionally or spiritually:

"We each had our own schedules, agendas, likes, and dislikes and never the twain met. Before we knew it, we were living together but rarely talking, never interacting—each of us with our own set ways—never compromising, never talking or laughing."

So what role does a social life play in all this? You may think it's not that important. After all, how can going to the movies, watching a play, or attending a football game together make a difference? Being social represents one spoke in a complicated network of activities, actions, and feelings that form your lives together. If one spoke weakens, the bike wobbles. If too many go bad, watch out: Collapse is looming. What are some of the obstacles that keep you from having a nice time together? Here are some of the main issues.

WHAT CAN COMPLICATE YOUR SOCIAL LIVES?

Husband-in-Front-of-the-TV Syndrome According to many women, this appears to be epidemic. It usually stems from boredom, depression, or just plain old selfishness. Of course it doesn't happen to just men. Watching TV all day (or an equally absorbing activity like playing video games or surfing the Internet) can be an excuse for not wanting to interact socially. This behavior—especially if it has recently started—is probably nothing more than avoidance.

Irresponsible Spending and Financial Disarray   Lack of discipline affects your ability to make important financial decisions together. The result will likely be less teamwork and fewer opportunities to enjoy one another socially. Review Chapter 4 for tips on taking control of your finances.

Time and Space Issues   These can be especially complicated after your first child is born. Time-management issues are at the center of many squabbles about personal freedom and space. Who owns what time? How can you make time to be by yourself to do the things you want to do? These issues threaten to split even the healthiest marriages. Later on, we'll take a look at ways to address these important and common problems.

Inflexibility   So you're used to staying up all night watching *The Late Show*—so what if your husband wants you to come to bed? Failing to alter some of your personal habits after you're married can hurt your relationship. It's nearly impossible to conduct your life as it was before. But if you're like most people, you need your own time. Read on.

Substance Abuse   This is a real, adult problem. This is not Hollywood. Substance abuse or excessive drinking will always come back (sometimes irreversibly) to damage your marriage, job performance, health, and family. Do not go another day without getting help. Ask your physician for a referral.

Moving   This will have a profound affect—at least temporarily—on your social life. Seek out relatives in the area, join a local community center, invite an old friend for a visit, and find out if there's a neighborhood welcoming organization. There's more on the complications of moving to a new town later in this chapter.

Having a Baby This is a huge—but wonderful—disruption of your social life. Dads, pick up a copy of *The Joy of Fatherhood* (Prima) for tips on how to make it through.

Marital Stress If you're arguing, maintaining your social habits is more difficult. Who wants to hang out with the "enemy"?

Job Stress This has a way of inhibiting your ability to have fun. People who bring their job issues home bring home anxiety and misery.

Minor Personality Differences Some people would rather stay home than go out. People who are very shy or withdrawn may feel very awkward among people they don't know. Unless you and your mate share this characteristic, the more gregarious one may become annoyed.

In marriage, things won't always be happening only to *you*. As we've already seen, they'll be happening to your family as well. But change will also affect your friends. How so? Well, if your emphasis is on you and your spouse—as it should be—your marriage may inexorably change the nature of the ways in which you relate to your old single friends. What can you do to prevent your friends from disowning you?

SINGLE FRIENDS MAY FEEL . . .

Envious Because of what you have: a new, permanent, legally binding arrangement with the partner of your choice. Friends may feel jealous or even competitive. These feelings can put a strain on your relationship:

"Since I got married, my friend is constantly telling me about her new boyfriend or all the new clothes she just bought. She doesn't talk about anything else. Gosh, she's annoying."

A Sense of Loss   Your friends will probably let you know, one way or another, that they feel a deep sense of loss as a result of your marriage—even if you still see each other regularly:

"My best friend—who happens to be my brother—seems so depressed since the wedding. He keeps saying it's nothing, but I know him far too well to believe it."

Uncomfortable   Even though you may have known each other for years, it wouldn't be uncommon for your best friend to act uncomfortable around you and your spouse:

"My girlfriend came over the other day. All she did was stand around and say, 'So . . . the married couple. Wow.' It was really uncomfortable for everyone."

"To me, getting married was the pinnacle of my career as a man. I really wanted to share it with my friends, but slowly, over time, they stopped coming around or even calling."

Abandoned   Your friends may feel left out, rejected, or given up on. They may also feel angry about, and even resentful of, your new role as husband or wife:

"My girlfriends seem perpetually upset with me."

Content   Most of your friends will continue to be good friends. Happy for you and pleased with your success as a husband or wife, they may be delighted to join with you in spirit as you make your way together:

FOCUS

Keeping Your Old Friends

Getting married is, of course, a wonderful and joyous event, but it can sometimes bring with it a sense of loss. Many newlyweds are unsure about how to include their old friends—some of whom may be single—in the new and intimate experience of being a married couple:

"My best friend has become so needy since I got married. She's single and has doubled her efforts to find a husband since I got married. I can't get off the phone with her."

You may ask yourself whether you'll be able to maintain friendships now that you're married. How will your single friends respond to your new lives together? As a married couple, the nature of your relationships may change dramatically:

"I had always had a ton of really close friends. We did everything together. These friendships survived my dating and even

"There's really nothing to report. It's really been business as usual. Our friends are still our friends."

In Denial Sometimes the "loss" of a friend to marriage can be too much to face:

"After the wedding, I never heard from my best man again."

So what's the best way to repair or maintain your friendships? Your new responsibilities as a marital partner will invariably take up a lot of

my engagement to my wife. But something happened after we got married. My friends stopped coming around. That made me sort of sad. I wasn't really sure what was going on. I mean, I really didn't have the kind of time I used to have, but still, I'd really hate to think that I've lost all these important people."

"I've just about lost my patience with my friends. They keep dropping over like nothing ever happened. They're starting to irritate me. I just don't have as much time to hang out with them as I used to."

Your worlds have changed—for the better in most cases. But what does that mean for you and those who came before your marriage? Although the changes that are taking place as a result of your union are far reaching, all is not lost! Marriage doesn't preclude having a great relationship with old friends. In fact, the chances are pretty good that your relationships will grow stronger and even more permanent. It may be helpful to take a look at some of your friends' reactions to your marriage.

your time, but don't forget that your social network is an essential component of your happiness. Remember to be sensitive to issues of loss and abandonment. Below are some suggestions to get things back on track and keep them there.

TO AVOID LOSING YOUR FRIENDS . . .

Don't Ignore the Problem   Try not to write off old friends. Instead, let them do what you've tried to do—grow accustomed to your new life slowly and gradually. Make an effort to make plans with them as often as your schedules permit—maybe half as often as you used to before you were married.

Be Together   To the extent it's possible, try to work through your friends' anxiety with them. Experience the uncomfortable disruption of new experiences together. If you sense your friends feel weird or anxious about your new status as a married couple, ask them about it. Tell them it will take some getting used to by everyone. Then make plans to do something together—and have some fun.

Include Them   Help your friends get acquainted with your new life by involving them in it. Include them in your new traditions, family holidays, or milestones in your marriage—like buying your first house or car.

Prioritize   Make your friends a priority, second only to your spouse. Shop, hang out, go to ball games, meet for dinner.

Communicate   While not a substitute for face-to-face meetings, telephone calls, e-mail, and letters help keep you in touch. Haven't had a good talk with your best friend lately? Invite him out or set up a time when you can talk.

Make a Schedule   With your husband's help, create a schedule—carve out time for your friends. Ask him to do the same.

In the long run, you'll be glad you took the time to nurture your "new" relationship with your old friends:

> *"After not having heard from our best friends for six months after the wedding, we bit the bullet and decided to call and invite them over for Christmas. I'm glad we did. We ended up talking all night. It was great! We discussed some of the issues that seemed to split us. Now we talk on the phone frequently. Just like old times."*

Being There for Each Other

Just because you're married doesn't mean you must spend every waking moment together. You can often avoid friction by respecting each other's social traditions, cherishing the time you spend together, and mastering the art of compromise. Time and space issues are frequently the root of petty arguments—and sometimes more serious problems—during the first year of marriage. Here are some things you can do to avoid stepping on each other's toes:

BE PATIENT

Everything worthwhile takes time. Remember that although you've probably known each other for years, being married is something completely different. It will take time for certain issues—including time and space conflicts—to emerge. When they do, go about the task of solving them lovingly and with patience.

DON'T SOLVE ALL THE PROBLEMS AT ONCE

Table the tough issues for later; solve the easy ones first.

ESTABLISH INDIVIDUAL SCHEDULES

Although flexibility in your relationship is admirable and desirable, a certain amount of structured time together is often necessary to establish flexibility. Get input from your other half and stake out the minimum amount of time to do the things you want to do on your own or with friends—staying up late watching reruns, shopping with a friend. Then . . .

ESTABLISH A JOINT SCHEDULE

Sit together and decide on what you want to do together over the next month or two—go to the movies, eat dinner out, stay home and talk. Don't skimp on the time you block off to spend together.

FOCUS

How to Increase Your Social Contacts

Making new friends is a little harder now that you're out of school, and if you've moved to a new city it can seem even more daunting. Here are several ways to add more names to your social calendar.

1. Get a job. While there are clearly other advantages to working—money and self-sufficiency—one of the nice side effects of work is a wider social circle. Since you'll probably know next to nobody if you move to a new city, this can be especially important for your and your partner's social lives.

2. Develop a hobby. Whether it's sewing, cooking, or collecting things, if you have a hobby and some extra time, try not to neglect it. Local organizations and events geared toward specific interests are everywhere. Check the local paper. People with the same passion are always looking for each other.

3. Take an adult education class. Who wants to go back to school? Well, it's not for everyone. Why go back? If you could learn to rebuild a car engine, learn therapeutic massage, improve

CHECK UP

Every month or so, check in with each other—go to dinner or just talk at home. Make sure you're still on the same wavelength.

RESPECT YOUR PARTNER

Don't belittle the way your husband or wife uses free time.

FIND COMMON GROUND

In time, if you've talked about your similarities and differences, you'll both probably find that you're spending quality time with each other, doing

your cooking skills, or study art history *and* meet new people at the same time, would it be worth your while? You can usually find adult ed or university extension classes at local high schools or community colleges. They tend to be inexpensive and just for fun. No SAT scores required!

4. Enlist your real estate broker. Brokers are especially helpful if you've just moved. Why not ask him or her to introduce you to local community members or suggest ways to meet people and places to go? You'll probably hit a jackpot of information.

5. Join a house of worship. Even if you're not religious, churches and synagogues usually have functions that draw a variety of people—religious and not. It's reasonably easy to meet new people and develop long-lasting friendships at such functions.

6. Encourage visits from friends. This is especially helpful if you have moved. You're not meeting new people, but seeing old friends can be comforting and fun. Reestablish ties with old friends with whom you have lost touch. Arrange to meet them halfway between their home and yours, or go away together. Spend a weekend together reminiscing.

(continued on next page)

things you both enjoy. Having "permission" from your husband or wife to go to the local *Star Trek* convention without being made fun of will actually increase mutual respect in your marriage. A little freedom goes a long way. Encouraging individuality often leads to common ground.

BE HONEST

Honesty works. If it's true, acknowledge that the proverbial honeymoon is over, and that you may actually not want to spend every waking moment together. Getting it out in the open will probably be a relief to both of you.

(Focus—continued)

7. Get in touch with nearby relatives. If you've moved, be sure to ask your relatives if you have any family in your new city. If you live near relatives you know of but have never met, give them a call and introduce yourselves. You may not end up wanting to see them frequently, but sometimes having family nearby can be comforting.

8. Talk to your partner. Take some time to catch up with your husband or wife. Find out how he's doing. Is she meeting people at work? Talk about what the two of you might do to increase your chances of meeting people.

9. Volunteer. Even if you have a full-time job, consider doing some volunteer work for an organization or cause you care about. In addition to providing a meaningful service, you'll also be out and about, meeting people and making friends.

10. Don't ignore your spouse's friends. They may have husbands or wives you could get to know—and like.

11. Buy a pet—because you love animals, want the companionship, and have the time, patience, and energy to be with it and care for it. A nice fringe benefit, however, is that pet owners come together at conventions or are members of organizations. Having pets in common is a great conversation starter.

12. Take walks. Provided that you live in a safe area, walking together in the evening is not only great exercise, but it's also a great way to meet other people. If you have a dog to walk, it's even easier.

13. Use your computer. While not everything to all people, and certainly not a substitute for real human face-to-face interaction, computers can sometimes help establish or reestablish friendships. Use a computer to e-mail old friends. Using reasonable caution, you can also meet others on the Internet who may share common interests.

14. Make friends at—or with—your hairdresser. Get a few good referrals for a beauty salon and make an appointment for a haircut or manicure. Once there, chatting with the hairdresser and other patrons can be an easy and natural way to make new acquaintances.

15. Establish traditions. Once you've established a few nice relationships, work together to nurture them. Establish regular traditions—weekend barbecues, holiday gatherings, annual concerts, and so on.

16. Rent or buy bicycles. Commit to using them weekly.

17. Join a gym or health club together.

18. Go rollerskating.

19. Join a local museum.

20. Switch hobbies—show each other how to do your favorite hobby.

21. Take a train trip into the country.

22. Go white-water rafting or canoeing.

23. Spend an afternoon at the music store, listening to and purchasing new music together.

24. Create a movie club with your friends. Everyone watches the same movie, then meets to discuss it.

25. Create a cooking club. Every month, one couple creates a theme dinner for the group.

26. Go camping.

27. Form a book club. Everyone reads the same book then meets to discuss it.

28. Have a theme party—'60s, '70s, jazz, and so on.

29. Go sledding.

30. Take advantage of other winter sports—go ice skating or cross-country or downhill skiing.

(continued on next page)

(Focus—continued)

31. Learn to water ski.

32. Take golf lessons together.

33. Pick an activity you've always dreamed of doing and take a private lesson together.

34. Attend craft shows.

35. Grow a vegetable garden together.

36. Form a co-ed softball or volleyball team with other couples and singles.

37. Play adult board games with your friends over champagne.

38. Use every opportunity to experience new things. Take advantage of your city's entertainment offerings—be aware of free or inexpensive events like fairs, parks, shows, and hobby or craft festivals.

It Just Keeps Getting Better

We've explored many variables that can bring pleasure to your lives together; these variables can also put a damper on your ability to have fun. We've also seen how important it is to have an enjoyable social life. It might be that, as a couple, you need to figure out how to increase your social contacts. This is certainly true if you've moved away with your spouse and have to start all over again. Sometimes getting into a rut socially can cause problems for newly married couples:

"Somehow, I thought that just being married would make things more exciting. It didn't."

The Focus section "How to Increase Your Social Contacts" (page 160), provides a variety of ways the two of you can expand your social circle.

Your Life Together

Establishing and maintaining friendships with others, as well as granting each other your own time and space, will ultimately strengthen your marriage. Your social lives—individually and as a couple—play an important role in the development of your marriage. In the next chapter, we'll continue to explore the practical and emotional aspects of your new lives together. If you've been married for six months or so, it's time to take an inventory of your lives. Are you growing together? How's the team doing? Are you both where you thought you'd be after six months of marriage?

· *9* ·

The Six-Month Checkup

HOW ARE YOU DOING SO FAR?

9

By the time the sixth month rolls around, most married couples seem to know the routine. After all, most newlyweds knew each other for quite a while before they were married. They have a sense of who they are, where they came from, and where they're going. Chances are you're both enjoying everything marriage and each other have to offer. Just the same, it's not a bad idea to take a closer look at yourselves. Although you may only have a few miles on your marriage, you still may need a minor tune-up.

So far, we've looked at some fundamental issues that face most newly married couples—family conflict, money, your first fight, keeping romance alive, and your social lives. Wrinkles in these areas, while common, can sometimes disrupt your lives, especially if they go unrecognized:

> *"We thought we had it all together, but there have been some nagging issues we haven't been able to even look at, let alone resolve. The funny thing is that they never really seemed all that obvious. They just kind of snuck up on us."*

The sixth month is a great time to take a look at these and other important issues. Why? You're only a little way into your marriage, but it's never too soon to make repairs or modifications. Couples maintain good marriages by stopping, looking, listening, reviewing, and regrouping. Getting stuck in a rut, even this early on, by establishing patterns that are disruptive or even uncompromising can still cause problems.

On the other hand, it is equally important to determine what *is* working for you. Building on that foundation while you're still learning to be with each other will help nurture a great marriage! This chapter will raise some interesting and important questions, which the two of you should be asking each other. What works? What doesn't? While we're at it, we'll also take a look at some ways you can establish healthy lifestyle choices together—eating right, exercising, and, after the drama of the wedding, maintaining what's left of your mental health.

What's New with the Two of You?

Since we've taken the time to stop off at the sixth month, let's review some basic but common feelings associated with the half-year mark. At this point, the feelings you experience as a result of being married vary a lot:

> *"It's been pure bliss. I love this man of mine."*

> *"It's been pure torture. I'd rather stick my finger in a toaster than stay married."*

> *"I'm intensely conflicted about the relationship. Sometimes it's good and sometimes it's not. Is that normal?"*

People's feelings fall all over the map. Here's an overview of some basic feelings you may be experiencing after being married about six months.

YOU MAY BE FEELING . . .

Completely Content. Wow!

> *"In my wildest dreams, I could not have imagined a more perfect relationship. Everything is going our way."*

The two of you must be doing everything right—fighting fair (or not at all), saving your pennies, spending enough time together, handling the relatives, and managing to stay head over heels in love with each other. Being totally content with your "mate for life" is admirable if not rare. Congratulations!

Happy—for the Most Part

By the sixth month, you should be able to glance back over your shoulders to see from where you've come. Most couples are pretty happy together, working through the tough times and enjoying the good ones:

> *"We have our issues. No surprises really. We talk, fight a bit, and make up. We love each other and are glad we got married. It's not perfect, but it seems like what life is all about."*

Couples in this category may have some questions, issues, and complaints, but seem to be able to work through them with minimal effort and a good attitude.

Delighted You Fooled Someone into Spending Eternity with You

Some people feel thankful to have found someone for life:

> *"I wake up every day and thank my lucky stars I'm not waking up alone."*

Thankful for the blessing of marriage and having found someone to share the trials and tribulations, most couples are content with their choices.

Ambivalent   Some people can't put a finger on exactly how they feel. And there's really nothing wrong with that:

> *"Most of the time, I'm delighted. Other times, I'm less than excited to be married to this inconsiderate oaf of a man."*

Depressed and Dissatisfied   For the small percentage of couples in this category, now's the time to act. As we'll see in Chapter 10, many things cause extreme unhappiness in a marriage, including infidelity, falling out of love, domestic abuse, substance abuse, and so on.

Having gone through some broad, descriptive categories, and since the two of you should always strive to improve things, what can you do to upgrade your marriage? Can you make it better? Let's find out.

Being There for Each Other

For the most part, if you've worked hard together to communicate your fears, constructively express your concerns, and celebrate your joys, chances are you're doing fine. By the sixth month, you probably both feel more secure in your respective roles in the marriage. You may even be able to detect or sense your partner's needs without having to ask or be told:

> *"Sometimes we can just look at each other and know."*

Your six-month anniversary is a great time to do an emotional reality check. Is marriage everything you had hoped for? Do you like the patterns that you have established so far? Is everything going the way you both would like? Are you moving forward? What's working? What needs improvement?

What about the rhythm, or routine, of your marriage? It's different for every couple. Is the routine getting dull or boring? Sometimes, married couples fall into such a fixed routine that they often miss out on important details, new experiences, or old traditions. Sometimes, being "perfect" has its drawbacks:

"I was doing my thing, she was doing hers. Before we knew it, things were going so well that we never even had to interact. It was really pretty bad. Who knew that 'perfect' could be so imperfect?"

Whether the marriage has you feeling content and happy, ambivalent or terrible, take a moment to step back a bit and watch yourselves from a distance. Try to see yourselves as others might see you. Don't lose sight of what's really happening. Take some time to observe the ways in which you interact with each other. Get it right now. Check up on yourselves and make changes if necessary. If you're both crawling through molasses, ask yourselves the following questions:

Six-Month Checklist

- *What has it been like to be married?* While the question sounds unusual, remember that you were probably wondering what it was going to be like to be married just six or seven months ago. Compare your answers. Try to be honest with yourselves. Has it been good to you? Are there parts about it that you don't like, or even hate?

"For the most part, my husband and I have been quite happy. The first few months were a bit rocky and I have to admit, I wasn't sure I wanted to stay with him. I think his adjustment difficulties were just as intense. We argued a lot over dumb things but when you're newly married and start fighting over things that don't seem that important, something is bound to give."

If you're unhappy, take the time to understand or identify the main problems and the ways in which your issues affect the relationship:

"We forced ourselves into a room one day, opened a bottle of wine, and just started talking about the tension. We decided we wouldn't leave until we got everything out into the open. Two bottles of wine later, we discovered that we were both feeling tense about a lot of different things—family, money, job insecurity—and didn't really know how to resolve the issues. Instead of working with each other or relying on each other, we turned on each other. Had we not discussed this, I hate to think what might have happened. After that night we decided to meet period-ically to prevent this sort of thing from happening again."

Don't forget that "mastering" marriage doesn't happen the second you say, "I do." It takes practice and experience. You can't automatically gain experience in something you've never done.

- *Have the two of you dealt constructively with your respective re-sponsibilities?* Do you each feel as though you're pulling your own weight? Do you share responsibilities well?

"This was a source of conflict for us. Despite the fact that we both worked, I was actually doing the majority of the housework, food shop-ping, bills, and caring for the house. Believe me, it bred a great deal of resentment. He said he made most of the money and was tired when he got home. I certainly made less money, but worked no less intensely and was burdened with the majority of the housework. I told him that the current arrangement was unacceptable. It took a few times, but I fig-ured that unless I hit him over the head with my unhappiness now, I'd be mopping the floors as an old lady while he drank beer on the couch. We decided to rotate the chores. He seems to do it more as a favor to me, rather than any sort of mutual commitment, but I guess it's a start."

Responsibilities tend to snowball as you move through different life stages—especially once you have children. Patterns you establish now, for better or worse, will most certainly follow you through life. Don't wait. Talk it out today.

- *Do you feel understimulated?* Feelings of boredom can lead to impulsiveness, irritability, poor communication, and lack of concern for one another. Who needs these feelings and behaviors in a marriage?

"After six or seven months, things slowed down. It was odd. We weren't 'just married' anymore, but we still had little formal experience with marriage. Like anyone else, we made lots of mistakes. All of a sudden, though, it got quiet—too quiet. We were so sick and tired of being with each other that we started to ignore one another. Soon we stopped talking. Before I knew it, I was out looking for 'attention' elsewhere. I caught myself though and went to my wife. I tried to remember with her all the great reasons we got together in the first place. We looked for common ground and ways to spice up our relationship—we started going out more, met people, and got excited about our youth, good health, and ability to treat ourselves every once in a while to extravagant things. We went away one weekend and were just completely self-indulgent. It seemed to work. We got it back."

You can easily overcome relationship roadblocks by using a few creative ideas to your advantage. Go away for a day trip. Stay at a cozy inn, even if it's nearby. Write down all the reasons you're together.

- *Have you considered making a few structural or procedural changes?* It may not seem like such a great idea, but altering your chores a bit can be helpful. If your wife does most of the cooking, prepare some meals and give her a break. If your husband fixes things around the house, learn to make some simple repairs. Variety is the spice of life. It keeps things lively and discourages boredom and rigidity.

- *How is your work life?* There's nothing like work and love to keep people happy, fulfilled, and fed. Are you working? Do you like your job? If not, do you bring home your anger, resentment, and unhappiness? If you bring it home now, you'll bring it home later—perhaps when you're a parent. Being angry all the time will not only make you sick, it will sicken those around you:

"Starting out your life is stressful enough—the relatives, money issues, and all. But there's nothing worse than being tortured at work and bringing your depression and desperation home with you. My wife had this 'great' job. It paid well and, in the beginning, she liked it. Then she got a new boss who treated her like garbage. He insulted her and belittled her work in front of her peers. He was gratuitously vicious. She'd come home in tears. But she felt like she couldn't quit because we needed the money. I told her that no amount of money was worth her getting sick. Although we didn't have a lot saved, we talked about the risks and benefits of her staying on versus quitting, and she decided to leave. I called my dad, who loaned us some money to get us through while she looked for another job. It might not have been the best way to do it, but we made the decision together and felt good about that. I'm certain our financial situation will be tough for a while, but it was such a downer having her suffer like that. To tell you the truth, it was upsetting me, too, because she seemed so distant and unavailable. Everything had to be focused on this one issue. Now we can really leave the office at five."

Sometimes it's necessary to bail out of a job quickly. For the most part though, unless you're independently wealthy, if you're thinking about a job change, approach it methodically. Don't leave on impulse. Have a plan. Study the job market first. Have some "I'm getting outta here" money saved, just in case you must leave abruptly. Get help from job banks—and certainly discuss it with your spouse. Like any other kind of stress, job stress can make you sick. If you find yourself desperately trying to climb out of an emotionally challenging rut at work, don't forget to take care of yourself.

- *Are you being good to yourselves?*

"As tough as things get in the marriage, financially, or on the job, I always make it a point to exercise at least three times each week. My feeling is that, in a way, the only thing we truly have control over is our bodies. When work gets too burdensome, or if I have a fight with my husband, I know I can always make myself feel better by working out. It boosts my self-esteem too. And my husband also likes the way I look, which is very important to me."

Don't forget that by taking care of yourself, you're taking care of your family.

- *How can the two of you learn to be more involved with each other?* Stop and think about your time together and time apart. Do your schedules make sense? Is there room for improvement or compromise? Are you both satisfied with your private time? Use creative solutions to solve tough problems:

"I used to be concerned about the ways we spent time together and apart. In the beginning, my husband still wanted an inordinate amount of time to himself. In fact, he used to fly to see his old friends and leave me at home. I protested, but he made me feel like there was something wrong with me—like I'm supposed to believe that every wife allows her husband to gallivant around the country. When it was time for me to travel to see my friends, he was less than enthusiastic. I really thought I knew this man. I told him that I was going to go see my friends anyway, but that if he'd like, he was welcome to join me. And so we started our 'every other month going away together to see friends club.' Eventually, we developed this great travel club—just us and our friends, going away for long weekends together, seeing the sights—each of us taking advantage of our freedom, friendship, and marriage."

A well-balanced routine makes sense. Just don't become rigid or set in your ways. Be sure to work out a schedule now. You'll avoid painful feelings and encourage warmth and fun.

- *What sort of tension has developed between the two of you?* At the six-month mark, you'll want to nip bad feelings in the bud. Don't wait. Ideally, your relationship is loving, supportive, and mutually satisfying. Also keep in mind that aside from your own personal happiness, you may one day have impressionable children. They'll learn the most about life from watching the two of you interact:

"It took me a while to realize that our behavior together was eventually going to be witnessed by who knows how many children. Since our wedding, although we love each other and have great respect and admiration for each other, we tend to resolve conflict through sarcasm and verbal altercation. In other words, the F-word flies around quite a bit. It's just the language we use to solve problems. A few insults here, a few there. We never mean it and always end up making up—but our future kids, of course, probably won't notice the making-up part. They'll just hear the yelling and swearing. We decided that we'd work on our fighting styles a bit—especially since we're planning to have children soon. We turned it into a game. Every time one of us uses the F-word, the other person charts it. Whoever says it the most at the end of the month has to clean the toilets."

If you two are squabbling often or seem to be in constant or episodic, but intense, conflict, now's the time to fix what's broken. Don't make an uneasy relationship the status quo of your time together.

- *Do you feel comfortable expressing both your pleasure and pain?* Aside from being able to discuss feelings you're clear and certain about, what about those that are less clear? There's nothing wrong with mixed feelings, especially when it comes to any number of important marital issues:

"My wife recently approached me about the possibility of 'expanding' the family, as she puts it. She was talking about having a baby of course. I told her that it was too soon—that we were still just getting to know each other. She didn't buy it, though, because we've known each other for seven years. We started talking more seriously about my doubts about having kids right now. I'm stressed at work, we have no money, and I'm really not sure that we've been married long enough. There are still things I want to do together without having to worry about raising a child. I also don't think I'm emotionally ready to be a father. Frankly, the concept scares me. As it turns out, she has fears too. So we've started a dialogue of sorts. Luckily, we both feel pretty comfortable talking about these issues."

Both of you should accept ambivalence and allow its expression. Remember, sometimes chaos can lead to great achievements and creativity.

- *Have you been able to identify things about your marriage that frighten, anger, or depress you?*

"Frankly, some of my husband's habits scare the hell out of me."

It sounds depressing, but it happens to all of us. There's certainly no such thing as a flawless, perfect relationship—but it can't hurt to try for one. Can the two of you identify and work toward resolving these issues in a calm, productive fashion?

"We have no problem voicing our disdain for each other's antics. But it can get pretty scary sometimes."

- *How involved are you?* Are you in tune with your husband's life? Are you up-to-date with your wife's life? There are some very definite warning signs that you're not involved enough: Do you know her boss's name? Can you recall your husband's last conflict at work? Are you remembering important holidays or special dates that are significant to your wife? If you've fallen behind, catch up by spending some time alone with each other. Ask questions.

After reviewing some of these issues together, pick one particular issue and spend some time talking about it in greater detail. If you discover wide areas of disagreement or controversy, ask yourselves what's causing it. Above all, don't wait for things to resolve themselves. They probably won't. By the time it's too much to bear, you'll both be sorry you didn't deal with the problems earlier.

Staying Healthy Together

Okay, after reading the last chapter, you started to look after your social lives a bit. Great! What's next?

"My wife always says I have 'reaped the benefits of her good cooking' this past year. I guess what she really means is that I've gained a bit of weight."

As the two of you travel through life together, much of what you'll bring along will have been stuffed into the symbolic suitcases during your first year of marriage. If your habits are good ones, you'll be far better off as you grow older together. If not—

"Do you mean I'm always going to look like this?"

No! Staying healthy doesn't mean that you have to pump iron daily, eat cardboard-flavored rice cakes, and swear off all the fun stuff. There's no point in going to extremes in the name of leading a healthy lifestyle:

"Who's got the time to exercise?"

And you don't need massive amounts of time.

Don't forget that "health" is a broad term. It implies physical as well as emotional well-being. Sometimes married couples fall into a pattern of mindless repetition or routine, which breeds boredom, inactivity, and contributes to lowering self-worth:

"I can see that right after the wedding, we became very settled. We rarely worked out. We were way too involved with our work. We ate a lot of fast food and started to lose a lot of the vitality that we used to have. After a while, we just sort of got depressed. Once you feel that way, it's really tough to get back into good habits."

Why take care of yourselves? For one reason, it's one of the best ways to fend off illness. Here are a few more reasons: If you don't do it for yourself, then do it for your husband or wife. Do you want him or her to be lonely without you? Surely you want your children to enjoy and learn from you for a long time. Staying physically healthy helps build a strong marriage. You'll save money and time. You'll feel good about yourself, and others will feel good about you. Your performance at work will improve. You'll have greater endurance—in every respect. You'll be a role model for your future children. Staying in shape is a nice way to be together.

So what does it take to maintain your overall health? Time, money, sore muscles? What about your mental health? Most couples can learn to have fun and get into reasonably good shape—physically and mentally—without having to make enormous sacrifices. Getting back on track takes small amounts of time, a bit of energy, and some structured activities. Following are some suggestions for getting started.

EAT WELL

A proper diet is, of course, only one part of a "stay healthy" plan. Nonetheless, it's an important one. One of the nice parts of being together, even if you've never cooked before, is that you can prepare meals together:

> *"I must admit, I had never peeled a carrot before. My wife and I decided to make some carrot soup together. I'm not a vegetable guy, but the stuff was great and we made it ourselves. While we prepared the food, we talked about our day. It was really effortless. I recommend it."*

Cooking together will bring the two of you closer. It will also make you appreciate how hard the other works in the kitchen while you're sitting on the couch watching tabloid TV.

EXERCISE

How important is exercise? Study after study reveals that moderate exercise extends life, helps you sleep better, reduces your need for caffeine and other artificial stimulants, and can prevent stress and depression. Some people cringe at the thought but they might not realize that they can work out together. And you don't have to kill yourself with the effort:

> *"My husband and I walk every morning before we go to work. It's easy. We get up a bit earlier. Walking gives us a chance to review the week, or talk about the future. It's good exercise and a great way to catch up with each other."*

Almost any activity or sport will provide you with exercise. Tennis, walking, swimming, in-line skating, jogging, martial arts, hiking,

> 🞉 Celebrate six successful months of marriage with a small party.

dancing, biking—almost anything (other than thumb wrestling). Build these activities into your schedule and make them an integral part of your lives together.

Exercise plays a crucial role in any overall health plan. It should be as much a part of your life as work and love. It enhances your self-image, relaxes you, releases tension, and helps create a healthy family system. You and your husband will grow closer as a result. Don't assume that you need to go to extremes. Begin a routine slowly. Do whatever you need to do to get it done.

MEDICAL ISSUES

Be sure to see your primary-care physician once a year for a checkup. To ensure early detection of potentially serious conditions, ask your doctor for advice about how to do routine self-exams. Although young people are generally healthy, it's never too soon to start falling into patterns that continue automatically as you get older.

HOBBIES

Distractions, skills, and hobbies are all vital. They help keep you together. Don't downplay or scoff at the notion of pure relaxation. If you once had a hobby you really enjoyed, get back into it. If you're looking to develop a new one, ask your friends what they do. Sharing hobbies with your mate can be fun too. How about something healthy? Grow a vegetable garden together. No yard? No problem. Grow a patio or container garden.

SEX

Don't let the excuse that you "don't have time" get in the way of a healthy sex life. There's always time for *that*. Some couples complain that sex was better before marriage, but don't let the fact that you're married stop you from carrying on the same way you used to. Sex offers an intense intimacy that is as important to a couple's mental health as anything we've discussed so far. Make sure your sex life is on track.

Make the Best of It When Your Spouse Travels

What sorts of feelings are common among the well-traveled? Interestingly enough, they usually share the same feelings with the ones who wait at home:

> *"I can tell you that both my husband and myself feel pretty bad about his constant traveling. It makes me very lonely. I worry about his safety—if he'll get into an accident or get mugged. I feel left out of his work life and resent his frequent trips out of state. Unfortunately, we're without many options at this point."*

Here's how you can make the best of a trying situation.

Discuss Your Mutual Feelings

If you are troubled, talk about it. When you finally settle down and communicate, you'll probably find that you feel the same way about many things, particularly being apart so much. Your mutual feelings

LAUGH

Couples who don't take themselves too seriously and are able to laugh at themselves tend to be emotionally healthier than those who are rigid and compulsive. Couples who use humor to help their marriages move along tend also to last longer. Be flexible, employ humor to resolve personal crises, and exercise restraint when debating a hot topic:

> *"We actually become very childish when we fight. We both end up pushing our noses up in the air and make pig faces at each other. Such maturity—but it's hard to be angry at a pig."*

may include estrangement, loneliness, boredom, resentment, and fear.

Travel Together Although it's not always logistically possible, consider traveling together once in a while. If the nontraveling spouse works, that person should take a day or two off and accompany the traveler on the next brief trip. See the local sights while the other spouse works.

Use Different Forms of Communication The phone is nice, but variety is the spice of life. If she'll be away for a long time period, give e-mail a try. You can send provocative pictures and messages to each other.

Better Yourself Don't just sit around waiting idly. If your husband's away and if you have the time, work out, start a hobby, go out with friends, study. Use the time to your best advantage.

(continued on next page)

While you don't need to keep your husband or wife rolling in the aisles, levity has its place. As you grow together, you'll eventually see that the issues that seemed so important—perhaps even divisive—when you were younger are all but a memory now. Time has a way of placing things in their proper context. You may eventually wish that your approach to conflict had been less intense.

SPEND TIME ALONE

If you're the sort of person who relishes private time, by all means make sure you get some:

(Focus—continued)

Be Understanding of Time and Space Issues You should both attend to these important concerns upon the traveling partner's return. She'll want time with you, of course, but may also need to relax by doing other things—alone or with friends. You'll want time with her, but if you've taken advantage of your free time while she was away, you'll recognize that she'll want some too.

Celebrate the Return Start a tradition. See a movie; go out to eat; have a small, intimate party for two.

"I often need to go out alone to clear my head, regroup, and get it together. I'm much more pleasant to be around. It's actually much better for the marriage. My wife understands completely."

Overcoming Your New Obstacles

You've made it through the rigors of the sixth-month checklist. What's next? Have we forgotten anything or anybody? What about couples who aren't able to spend much time together? How do they manage? It seems like more and more people have to hit the road to make ends meet:

"My husband is on the road three weeks out of every month. Maybe that's why our marriage is so good."

For many couples, having one partner away from home a lot doesn't seem that advantageous at all:

"I can't remember what he looks like half the time. I hate sleeping alone, and I get scared sometimes. What happens when we have kids? Who's going to be their father? Did we get married just so we could be apart?"

Whether you're away selling pork-belly futures, insurance, imitation designer watches, or computer systems, being away from home can be difficult and leads to a variety of undesirable side effects. What can the two of you do to lessen the strain? How can you make the best of a tough but necessary situation? In the Focus section "Make the Best of It When Your Spouse Travels" (page 184), we'll look at what it's like when one spouse is on the road and the other is stuck at home alone.

Your Life Together

You've made it to the halfway point. Thanks to your dedication to the marriage, respect for each other, patience, compromise, and creativity, you're learning how to grow *together*. If you've been paying attention to the positives in the relationship, you'll be able to capitalize on them and continue to employ skills you've learned along the way to make the second six months even better. Likewise, there's no shame in acknowledging weaknesses in the way the two of you interact with each other. Now's the time to fix them.

You should think about yourselves too—particularly your health and how to maintain it. You'll need to expend a little energy to stay fit, but the benefits are enormous. Using common sense and making healthy lifestyle choices gives you more control over your lives. But what if things go terribly wrong? What then? In the next chapter, we'll explore irreconcilable differences—differences that threaten not only the integrity of your marriage, but your personal happiness, and even your health.

· 10 ·

Making It Work

HOW TO AVOID THE CRUMBLING MARRIAGE

10

As we have seen, marriage typically opens up new and exciting opportunities for self-growth, intimacy, and sustained friendship. The first year is a great time to try new things with each other, explore your feelings and attitudes, and provide a loving atmosphere in which you both can grow. Sometimes, though, a marriage can hit a snag or bump in the road, forcing couples to rethink their roles in the relationship.

What causes the "bumps in the road"? How should you deal with them? Do they happen suddenly? Will problems in the marriage lead to greater future difficulties—separation or even divorce? For the most part, a lot of what could be described as tension in the marriage seems to be temporary. With a bit of love, attention, and hard work, most newlyweds *do* make it to the next year together! In this chapter, we'll take a look at the "bumps." As we'll see, recognizing the strengths and weaknesses of your relationship will go a long way toward preventing problems or repairing them should they occur. We'll also explore some ways the two of you can work toward happiness in your marriage.

What's New with the Two of You?

Sometimes, despite their best efforts, two people living together just can't get along all of the time. Try not to worry! Over the years, you'll undoubtedly have your share of disagreements, ambivalent feelings, and uncertainty. For many couples, tough times will be limited to the occasional blowout or periodic argument—common in most every marriage. But there's a difference between episodic problems and the sorts of behaviors, attitudes, and issues that can eventually lead to a more sustained problem:

> *"It happened slowly, over time. We started talking to each other rudely, with little regard for each other's feelings. Eventually, we just stopped talking altogether."*

There's nothing particularly glaring or predictable about stressed marriages. In fact, it can be tough to pick up on the warning signs.

A moment in a day in the life of a struggling married couple will likely not reveal any obvious signs or symptoms of failure. Is there a final common pathway? With some exceptions, the slow crumbling of a marriage can generally be attributed to insidious, gradual erosion of respect for each other accompanied by the loss of perspective. These losses are powerful and chew away at the fabric of a marriage.

Why Does Marriage Falter?

LOSS OF RESPECT

The gradually growing distance between husband and wife can usually be attributed to loss of respect for each other. This largely occurs as a result of many problems compounded over time: taking yourselves too seriously, not compromising, failing to listen to each other, not sharing responsibilities, forgetting to appreciate your differences and instead using them as a wedge, not respecting time and space issues, and being inconsiderate:

> *"We started out our marriage as most others do. We were idealistic, in love, and kind to each other. After a series of petty arguments, none of which were resolved in an appropriate fashion, we started noticing vast differences in the way we related to each other. We were always snapping at each other, we lost our senses of humor, and we couldn't agree on even the simplest issues. We dug in and refused to alter our own perception of what was important to us."*

Be especially aware of the ways in which you use anger, language, and each other's past personal history:

> *"It all started innocently enough—disagreements, then arguments, and finally yelling and insulting each other. It just got way too out of hand."*

FALLING OUT OF LOVE

Nobody understands just how it happens, but occasionally it does. There are many different circumstances under which this might occur. Sometimes the feeling is mutual, but more often one person starts to feel uneasy about his or her love for the other. Would a longer courtship or engagement have helped? In some cases, maybe. But for the most part, falling out of love is something that doesn't seem to have a rhyme or reason. How about the loss of physical attraction? Now there's a confusing problem. And while each particular case is different, a lot of the time it has more to do with the fulfillment of one's own selfish needs and personal insecurities.

INSENSITIVITY AND LACK OF MOTIVATION

Some people just can't accept the notion of sharing life together, working as a team, or suspending their personal agendas, at least temporarily, for the good of the relationship.

FOCUS

The Truth About Infidelity

There are many tough issues that surround infidelity, some of which are matters of opinion: Are affairs ever justified? Can marriage ever be the same if one party has had an affair? Are affairs inevitably the result of the complex psychological dynamic between husband and wife? Does the person engaged in an affair have sole responsibility for that affair?

And affairs don't just go on between beautiful Hollywood types. The truth is that you can be as homely as a troll and still get caught up in an extramarital affair. What are the circumstances? How does it happen? Some marriages start off badly—and go downhill from there. Whether it's the result of the wrong fit, an impulsive marriage, or just a bad choice, getting off to a bad start does happen. The commitment of marriage must be taken seriously. Spouses who don't cherish the institution usually make bad life partners.

One spouse may be unfaithful—seeking love, satisfaction, or companionship from another person or a number of other people. Or promiscuity may be an issue. Most of the time, people

LOSS OF SHARED BELIEFS

Very few couples start out believing that their differences will one day divide them. When the subject of children, jobs, lifestyles, and places to live come up, some couples can't agree on anything:

> *"I couldn't believe my husband when, all of a sudden, he told me that he would never entertain having children. I thought we knew each other and held clear, common core beliefs."*

who have a history of sexual promiscuity before marriage settle in after marriage and become devoted spouses. However, promiscuity may also continue in the form of repeated affairs. Certain personality problems may be connected to promiscuity as well.

What are some other precipitants? Unfortunately, when you've lost respect for your spouse, either or both of you are more likely to seek affection from other people. Before you act hastily, keep in mind that the illusion that sex with someone else will somehow make things better invariably backfires.

Low self-esteem often compels people to try to compensate by doing or saying things they otherwise wouldn't. Often people who are considering having an affair may be experiencing a particularly stressful or depressing period, which may have damaged their self-worth. Affairs, in this case, are really nothing more than "happy pills" designed to bolster sagging self-esteem. In the end, of course, these people are far worse off.

Some people claim that they've had affairs because of an abundance of potential partners in their place of employment, for example. In this case, it's likely that there are other underlying issues. Sudden changes in a person's attitude toward sex, romance, or friendship in his or her marriage may lead that

(continued on next page)

RELIGIOUS AND CULTURAL DIFFERENCES

Despite the true love that initially overshadowed important differences between the two of you, there *are* significant difference between cultures that can interfere with your ability to stay together. Sometimes the differences are too much to bear—and they usually come to a head in the context of pregnancy and childbirth. Two people of different religions or cultural backgrounds sometimes have trouble resting on common ground when it comes to establishing a cultural identity for their children.

(Focus—continued)
person to consider an affair. The withholding of sexual intimacy, usually for extended periods of time, signals a more complex problem. Affected couples should consider counseling or psychotherapy.

People list many other reasons for having affairs, most of which deal with a person's unconscious motivations. The reasons range from self-destructive impulses and sadistic urges to fear of commitment and the need to fulfill infantile or primitive psychological desires and instincts. Sometimes, unfortunately, psychological theory becomes an excuse for bad behavior; however, an explanation or excuse doesn't make it right.

Affairs have so many negative consequences, it's hard to understand why they happen. What consequences? Affairs shut people up. If one of you is having an affair, you're doing, not talking. Affairs abruptly stop real dialogue between couples. They spread disease, destroy families, cheapen your reputation,

PERSONALITY PROBLEMS

Some people's personality styles make them very difficult to live with:

"My wife is very sensitive—complaining about me if I don't give her my full attention all the time. She threatens to leave if she feels I've slighted her in any way. But then she comes back sobbing and clinging to me. Her moods are extremely variable—happy one minute, depressed the next. I can't take it anymore. I love her, but what a position to be in."

A personality disorder describes a set of behaviors or attitudes that adversely affect the way some people interact with the world. Certain personality problems are characterized by perpetual dishonesty, anger, and lack of empathy or conscience. There are also those who may worry

humiliate your spouse, induce guilt, do not set a good example for children, make a poor substitute for personal growth and self-expression, and shatter trust.

Ideally, a marriage should never get to this point, but in an impassable situation affairs *can* be ice-breakers. That is, for a couple who have grown so far apart, the discovery of an affair tends to force them to make some important decisions, and puts pressure on them to solve the problem. Sometimes couples are able to get past an affair, fix the underlying problems, and grow stronger because of it. But having an affair is certainly not a recommended way to get your marriage back on track!

How can you prevent infidelity? Since affairs are really a symptom of a broken marriage, the focus should be on maintaining a healthy relationship in the first place, respecting each other throughout your marriage, and working together to prevent issues that lead to infidelity.

constantly about their appearance—to the exclusion of caring about anything or anyone else. Others are quick to judge, excessively dependent, ruminative, pathologically shy, or extremely dramatic and selfish.

People who suffer from certain forms of mental illness may require repeated psychiatric hospitalizations. The time, expense, and change in the affected person's personality can severely stress a marriage. Frequently, spouses need support too, even counseling, to help deal with their mixture of intense feelings.

INFIDELITY

Cheating tears holes in the fabric of trust and confidence. Most people find infidelity intolerable. Some couples are able to work through their issues and persevere. Sometimes if the overall marriage is

FOCUS

How to Repair Your Relationship
Before It's Too Late

If you take stock of your marriage and feel uneasy about it
after reading this chapter, consider the following questions:

- *Is there a problem?*
- *Can you identify the specifics of the problem?*
- *Are both of you willing to take a hard look at the issues?* Do you
  both believe a problem exists? If not, can you weigh the pluses
  and minuses of remaining in the relationship, given your particular set of circumstances?
- *What role does anger play in your problems?* If either of you has
  gotten to the point where you've tried to reduce your expression
  of anger, felt angry when those around you mention your anger,
  or experienced significant guilt feelings about your anger, you
  may need to examine treatment options more carefully. If you
  have trouble saying you're sorry or if you feel as though you're
  never wrong, it may be time to take a look at yourself more
  closely. If your anger frightens those around you, leads to physical
  assaults or destruction, or interferes with your or your partner's
  functioning, get help now. Ask your doctor or clergyperson for a
  referral to a good psychologist or counselor.

poor, one or sometimes both people will seek outside companionship in the form of sex.

There are many reasons that people have affairs. Sometimes
one partner will have a sexual encounter outside the marriage out of
curiosity, selfishness, or hostility toward their spouse. Some people

- *Do you believe you're both responsible for the problems?*
  Remember, it generally takes two to generate marital problems.
- *Do you want to stay together?*
- *Can you forgive your mate's errors of judgment or transgressions?*
  Under what circumstances?

Once you've answered these questions, you'll likely want to act on what you've found out. Before we give suggestions for what you *should* do, here are some things to avoid doing. **Do not:**

- *Bury your head in the sand:* Your problems will not go away. If they do, they will always return—but they'll be bigger and more intense. Unresolved issues will haunt you and could eventually ruin your marriage. Don't neglect them. Act now.
- *Become destructive, apathetic, or intoxicated:* Don't allow your problems—even if they are serious—to get the best of you. Stay healthy and remain devoted to your resolution either through teamwork, or by way of an attorney.
- *Expect your partner to take care of the problem for both of you:* It's both your problem. If you hear or say, "She can go to therapy and work it all out, if she wants," you're headed in the wrong direction.

Here are some things you can do to start fixing the things that are broken in your marriage—a list of do's. *Do:*

(continued on next page)

will create issues that may or may not exist as an excuse to cheat: not liking their spouse's appearance or being upset over a perceived slight, for example. Also, the notion of an "open marriage" (marriage with additional sexual relationships with the people of your choosing), while sometimes an enticing and exciting fantasy, is nonetheless

(Focus—continued)

- *Solve the problems together:* Marriage, by definition, is a two-person event.
- *Obtain counseling:* Ask your primary-care physician or a trusted friend for the names of a few different therapists. Therapy need not be excessively time-consuming or expensive. And remember that couples therapy is not a guarantee that your marriage will survive. In fact, a good therapist will make no claims about saving your marriage. Treatment usually centers on identifying or clarifying important and divisive issues, which allows both of you to overcome resistance to grappling with these issues. With this information, the two of you can make an informed decision about whether to remain married. Sometimes separation and divorce are the best choice. You don't want to ruin your lives by staying together if it's not the right thing to do.
- *Avoid the all-or-nothing approach to reconciliation and treatment:* A marriage is a work-in-progress—and so is fixing it. If you've decided to hang in there and work together, be patient and accept uncertainty. You'll be better off.
- *Check with your doctor:* More than ever before, a variety of medications for impulsiveness, anger, and depression are

destructive. It will not set the stage for a stable family or marriage. See the Focus section "The Truth About Infidelity" (page 194), for a closer look at this subject.

Being There for Each Other

Unfortunately, if you're reading this chapter, it's possible that you two haven't really "been there" for each other, or are seriously considering "not being there" in the future. Nonetheless, there's still hope for you. We've

readily available. If any of these conditions affect your life and/or relationship, consider judicious use of medication. Check with your primary-care physician for the medication that best suits you.

- *Use healthy outlets.* You should have personal time, space, hobbies, friends, and the opportunity to exercise regularly. These activities need not be expensive or time-consuming, but they are essential for the maintenance of your mental health.

- *Consider separation as an alternative to remaining painfully together and/or divorce.* A lot of good therapeutic work can take place in the context of separation—work that is impossible while you're under the same roof. Very often, separation leads to a reapproachment.

What if your marriage has passed the point of no return? Nobody likes the thought of divorce. After all, it signifies a failure of sorts. And the thought of starting all over again can be equally as painful. Keep in mind that many couples separate, divorce, and still go on to have wonderful lives, happy relationships, and satisfying marriages.

already seen what sorts of issues, conflicts, and problems can cause glitches in the "system" as we travel down the road of marriage. Depending on your particular set of circumstances, some may be reparable. See the Focus section "How to Repair Your Relationship Before It's Too Late" (page 198).

Your Life Together

As we've seen, nothing good can come from ignoring a bad situation. We hope the two of you will never need to study this chapter intensively.

Always keep in mind that happiness in marriage doesn't preclude an occasional confrontation. It's up to both of you to determine if your problems are sustained and emotionally destructive or episodic and within normal limits. Staying happy and healthy is what it's all about.

· 11 ·

Planning for Parenthood

HOW TO TELL IF YOU'RE READY

11

It seems like only yesterday that you were dancing at the wedding, honeymooning, squabbling with your in-laws, or having your first big fight. A lot can happen in less than a year. Things have certainly changed! As you've journeyed together through a variety of new trials and tribulations, learning to grow together, you've undoubtedly started thinking realistically about other things:

> *"Our marriage is really tight. We communicate well, have great respect for each other, and love spending time together. We've recently started talking about having children. I can't remember a more exciting time."*

Of course, discussing parenthood is serious stuff, but you'll undoubtedly have the time of your life toying with the idea:

> *"My husband and I just look at each other and giggle every time we talk about babies. It just seems like a dream to us—you know, that we'll be parents soon."*

While deciding to get married took time, discussion, a degree of courage, and love, talking about starting a family is unlike anything you've ever experienced together. It will be a time of personal reflection, joint decision making, intimacy, and, to some degree, anxiety:

"I guess I was in a state of denial. I didn't really think it was an option. It seems like such an 'adult' thing to do. Somehow I had forgotten that we don't need permission to go ahead with it. I'm really excited about it."

After a year or so of marriage, the "baby talk" is almost inevitable for most couples. Because everyone is different, your excitement may be dotted with a bit of uncertainty as well. How could it not be?

You may feel excited about the prospect of having a baby, but if you're like most people you may feel nervous as well—especially when you stop to consider the impact a baby will have on your life. How will you deal with it? How will the two of you approach your discussions, points of view, and plans? What sorts of things are running through your heads? Why worry?

There will be issues that you need to sort through *before* you conceive a child. Giving them consideration now, before the two of you act, will give you an opportunity to think out loud about a decision that will have incredible, lifelong implications. In this chapter, we'll take a look at some of the things you might want to consider before deciding to have a child. We'll also explore reasons *not* to get pregnant right now, as well as great consequences of having a baby.

What's New with the Two of You?

While there's nothing quite like having a baby, there's also nothing quite like the feelings, thoughts, and ideas that accompany the decision-making process. Confusion about parenthood can be a good thing:

"We really struggled with the decision. I mean, there are so many things to consider. I feel like we've talked it out and are better off for our efforts."

People usually run through an entire spectrum of feelings about having children. You'll both probably be relieved to learn that there are no right or wrong feelings. Each spouse will invariably have his or her own way of perceiving the phenomenon of parenting.

YOU MAY BE FEELING . . .

Excited and Overjoyed   What's not to be excited about? After all, your decision to have a baby signifies an entirely new step in your lives together. It says something about you, your commitment to your marriage, and your ability to communicate with your spouse. For some couples, pregnancy is the sum total of all their experiences, love for each other, wishes, hopes, and desires:

> *"To my way of thinking, having a baby really symbolizes everything I've ever wanted, and with the person I've always wanted to have it with."*

Anxious   Anxiety is a universal feeling. There's no more appropriate time to feel anxious than when discussing babies:

> *"I'm overwhelmed by a sense of doom and terror—and those are just* my *positive* feelings.*"

Given the enormity of your potential responsibility, there's nothing wrong with feeling nervous.

Complete   For some couples, having a child is the final step in cementing their lives together:

> *"This is what we have always wanted for each other. It makes us feel whole."*

Grown-Up   Although courtship and marriage were stops along the way, having a baby, for some, signals the end of an era and the beginning of a new one:

> *"There's something very grown-up about having a baby. It's almost like before this, I was a kid."*

Ambivalent Is it possible to be excited, happy, and anxious all at the same time? Sure—it's called ambivalence:

> "I'm happy about our decision to discuss it but at the same time, I'm completely freaked-out . I'm not at all comfortable with this mixture of feelings."

Have no fear! Most people feel a variety of sometimes conflicting feelings about any number of things. Having mixed feelings about something as important as parenting signals thought, not action. And there's nothing wrong with that.

Pressured Feeling pressured to have a baby is not a great way to get started:

> "Everyone is pushing us to get pregnant for the dumbest reasons. We can't stand it. These decisions are personal and no one else's business."

Fearful It's not uncommon for couples to feel frightened or apprehensive about a host of important issues related to parenting. Some couples are afraid that they won't have the patience or the "right" personality type for a baby. Others fear losing their free time. We'll take a look at these important considerations in greater depth later in this chapter.

Does talking about having a baby sound confusing? Well, it can be. Don't worry. You'll definitely get through it one way or another. But what about a situation where the two of you are not seeing eye-to-eye? What about your differences? Let's take a look at how differences sometimes play out.

Being There for Each Other

Part of learning to live and grow together as a married couple comes in rejoicing in your differences. There will be times when you don't agree on some pretty important issues. Having a baby is often the focus of heated debate—much of which is really about the resolution of anxiety caused by your differences. What are some of the issues and how can they be brought out into the open? Let's explore the possible differences between you and your spouse.

SHE MAY BE THINKING ABOUT . . .

Physical Changes   Sometimes issues related to the pain of childbirth, the physiological changes in their bodies, the biology of childbirth, and the neonatal period may influence a woman's decision-making process.

Responsibility   Regardless of whether Mom will be working outside at her regular job or staying at home, she'll undoubtedly be thinking about the tremendous responsibilities that accompany childbirth:

> *"I'm overextended as it is."*

Some women may even question their mothering abilities, fearing the awesome responsibilities that accompany having a child. They may also be concerned with how they'll balance time with their babies and their husbands.

Career   Somewhere in her thoughts about children will very likely be some anxiety in regard to balancing roles of mother and professional person. Some women, if they decide to leave work outside of the home to raise children, may mourn the potential loss of their jobs or may simply fear loss of freedom.

Her Mother   Some women will compare themselves to their mothers:

> *"When we started to talk about getting pregnant, I automatically thought about my mother at my age. You know, what she was thinking or feeling. I bet she was thinking about her mother."*

While you may have mixed feelings about your mom, you'll undoubtedly try to use the positive mothering skills she used to help raise you.

Her Husband   How will your husband react to the baby? Will he have enough time to be a father? What kind of father will he be?

HE MAY BE THINKING ABOUT . . .

His Dad   Just as women's thoughts turn to their mothers, so too do potential dads think about their fathers. It's very common for men to think about fatherhood in terms of their own paternal role models. Men's feelings about their own fathers range from panic to thoughtfulness:

> *"Dad tried his best. I think all in all, I'd probably like to be like he was."*

If you're like most people, you'll have many different feelings about your dad. Most men make an attempt to be as competent at fathering as their own fathers, but also may fear emulating behavior they don't approve of.

Time   It's hard not to consider this. In fact, many men worry that they'll be unable to juggle the responsibilities of fatherhood with work and play:

> *"How am I possibly going to be a good father, husband, and employee?"*

His Lack of Fathering Experience   Some men feel somewhat alienated from the process. Believing that women become good mothers naturally, or that they somehow are born to know what to do with a baby—how to hold or feed it, for example—many fathers-to-be voice apprehension about their role:

> *"I'm petrified. I don't know anything about babies. My wife's been reading books, but somehow I feel like she already knows how to be a great mother."*

Regardless of your gender, there's no way either of you can be experienced in something you have not experienced together. For the most part, you'll learn the most by running *together* toward the inexperience and uncertainty. Don't pressure yourself to know everything, feel everything, or feel nothing. Since confusion and indecision lead to dialogue, you'll have far more to gain through uncertainty than through complete clarity.

Overcoming Your New Obstacles

Some people will spend more time discussing what brand of TV to buy than they will about pregnancy and it's lifelong implications. Fortunately, most couples will resolve their issues reasonably and go on to have children, wait to have children, or decide parenting is not for them. Some, unfortunately, ignore the negative possibilities and go ahead with having a child anyway.

Part of your decision-making process should focus on the risks and benefits of having children. Take the time now to weigh out the pluses and minuses of having a child. Most people know all the right reasons to have a baby. But there are reasons *not* to have children.

ELEVEN WRONG REASONS TO HAVE A BABY

1. You're bored or lonely. Don't rely on a newborn to provide you with psychotherapy. Try buying a puppy—or seeking counseling.

2. You want to save your marriage. For couples whose marriage is anything but secure, a child will only complicate matters. Sometimes the baby is the target of resentful feelings, especially if its intended purpose—to heal the marriage—was unsuccessful. Try to remember that your children will learn much about life and the world through observations of the two of you. Lack of love in your relationship will show up

FOCUS

Fourteen Great Consequences of Having a Baby

Thinking about babies? Need some compelling reasons to help you make up your mind? The most fabulous part of having a baby is love—pure and simple: love for your spouse, love for yourself, and love for your baby. There are other issues to be considered as well. In fact, having a baby engenders in most people a variety of special, even magical, feelings that can't be found under any other circumstance. Here are some terrific consequences of having a baby:

1. You'll better yourself through patience.
2. You'll enhance your teamwork skills.
3. You'll feel alternately youthful, exhausted, and invigorated.
4. You'll learn a lot.

later on in your children. A stable, not faltering, relationship is a prerequisite for having children.

3. You are trying to find yourself. Some people agree to have children because they think the experience will somehow transform their emptiness into completeness. Of course, having a baby can do that. But if your sole reason for having a child is so you can work on personal identity issues, chances are great that you'll end up a parent but still searching for your identity.

4. You plan to create a genius. In her book *The Drama of the Gifted Child,* (Translator), author Alice Miller discusses the way certain selfish parents try to live out their fantasies of success and accomplishment through their children—pushing them to perform without mercy—and in doing so ruin their children's life by making them feel loved and valued

5. You'll learn to be great with your hands—changing diapers is an art!

6. You'll achieve personal growth and self-improvement through self-sacrifice.

7. You'll get to hold (frequently) a little tiny person who looks like you or your mate.

8. You'll learn new and creative ways to manage your time.

9. You'll learn to give and share.

10. You'll become a teacher.

11. The concept of love, being loved, and being in love will never be clearer.

12. You'll learn to smile broadly, even when you're exhausted.

13. You'll get to watch those late, late, late shows on TV you were always curious about.

14. You'll love and appreciate your spouse in new ways because the two of you worked together on this beautiful creation.

only for what they can do, not for who they are. There's nothing wrong with wanting the best for your baby, but if your only goal is to create some sort of child prodigy, think again. Such behavior is a form of abuse.

5. You hate your job and are looking for something else to do. Don't give up your job just to have a baby. That's not a good enough reason.

6. You selfishly expect advantageous changes in your lifestyle. Trying to improve your social lives is not a good reason to have a baby. It clearly may be a wonderful fringe benefit, but it should not be your main focus.

7. You want to please your spouse or relatives. We all frequently do things solely to elicit praise from people who are important to us. However, bringing a life into the world to reap the rewards of a pat on the back hardly qualifies.

8. You need a tax deduction. Yes, it's a nice fringe benefit of parenthood. But believe me, any money you save on your taxes will be more than made up for with baby expenses.

9. You feel it's the natural progression of your marriage. The natural progression of your new marriage should be continuous dialogue about any number of things, not the least of which is a baby. There's no natural progression or mandatory next step.

10. You want to give your spouse a "reward." Buy her a necklace instead. Don't use a baby as a token of your appreciation.

11. You want to use pregnancy as a bargaining chip. Bartering a baby for other "goods" is not a good idea:

"I figured if I gave her a baby, she'd let me out of the house every once in a while."

It's important to realize that some of these feelings, thoughts, problems, and ideas may be temporary. That is, they may be issues now, but you will resolve them in time through dialogue. If the matters are pressing and you're unable to resolve them on your own, consider couples therapy or individual counseling. Ask a trusted friend or your physician for a referral.

Now that we've reviewed some reasons not to have a baby, what's next? It's time take a look at some "are you ready?" issues.

It Just Keeps Getting Better

What sorts of considerations should you look at when pondering pregnancy? Are there any magic key words or questions?

"Quick, somebody tell me what to do."

Since having a child will inexorably alter your lives, it makes sense that both of you be as involved in all aspects of the decision-making process as possible. Marriages can falter a bit after the birth of a child for many different reasons. So it's best to be prepared for some of the possibilities. Of course you love each other, but is that all that's important? While there are no right or wrong answers, maintaining a dialogue is crucial. After all, you thought long and hard about what kind of refrigerator to buy. Now it's time to give the same consideration to having a baby.

SHOULD WE HAVE A BABY?

Before you can answer that question, ask yourself these questions first:

- *Is your marriage intact?* This is crucial because having a new baby in the house can severely test a marriage. You may find yourselves feeling tired, irritable, sleep-deprived, sexually turned off, anxious, and depressed—all quite common temporary feelings for new parents. If your marriage was on shaky ground to start with, though, you're in for some trouble.

- *Do you have a place to live?* What a silly question, or is it?

"We weren't very settled in a place before we had our baby. We actually had to move from apartment to apartment for various reasons. It was very disruptive to the baby's schedule, and increased the level of stress between me and my husband."

We're not saying you need to own a home or even live in a house to have a baby:

"I grew up in an apartment and so did my husband. My baby seems no worse off for the experience to date."

But if you know you're going to be uprooted and moving frequently, it's probably best to wait until you have a permanent place—be it an apartment or house—that you can call your own.

- *Are there friends or relatives nearby?* While clearly not a prerequisite (some couples are delighted to leave their families behind), it's nice to have some family support during the first year of your baby's life:

"During the first few months, our baby cried constantly—actually, we all cried—no matter what we did. I was so completely stressed out that I wanted to scream—and get out of there. It would have been nice if my folks lived nearby (at least for a few months). My wife and I could have gone out once in a while and left the little critter with them."

Having family around to go gaga over the new addition is nice too:

"It pleases me to no end to see my parents swooning over the baby."

- *What will happen to your social lives?* It's important to consider a baby's impact, at least initially, on your social lives. A baby brings with it physical and emotional demands:

"If this child doesn't sleep once in a while, I'm going to shrivel up and die."

🐞 Take a vacation together to discuss your plans and share your philosophies about child-rearing. You may not have much time to yourselves after your baby's born—at least for a while.

Having a baby is a wonderful experience and as you watch him grow, you'll be rewarded many times over. The first year, however, can challenge even the most patient of parents. Chances are, you'll have to put your social lives on hold—at least temporarily. If you're having trouble accepting that fact, it may not be the right time to have a baby.

- *Is your financial situation stable?* Princes and paupers alike have had babies for thousands of years. Do you need to be loaded to be a great parent? Of course not. But there are some financial realities you must face. First of all, you'll need health insurance to cover your entire family. Your baby will have nutritional requirements (formula and baby food, for example), medical expenses, and other needs like toys, a crib, a nursery, clothing, and a variety of seldom-planned-for, unexpected expenses.

Child-care expenses alone can be overwhelming. Have you and your spouse decided on work schedules? Will you both work? If not, will you stay home? Try to work these details out now, before you get pregnant.

If you're out of work, or in a precarious financial position, it's probably best to wait. Believe me, you'll avoid conflict and heartache later on.

- *Have you defined your goals for the future?* If so, you may need to "undefine" them or at least redefine them. Having babies has an uncanny way of changing people's lives.

Your lives will be permanently altered (almost always for the better). But plans, notions, schemes, and ideas you had before the baby will probably have to change. You'll have less time and energy. If you want to be an active, involved parent, you need to rethink your ideas about such things as free time, private time, personal space, peace and quiet, and even personal hygiene:

"I don't even know what day it is. Who has time to bathe?"

Don't forget that the changes in your lives will be both far-reaching and fabulous. If you're the kind of person who can't envision giving something up to gain something wonderful, having a baby, at least right now, may not make sense.

- *How will your baby impact your lives together?* It's important to consider that having a baby—adding a third spoke to a previously two-spoked relationship—will change the dynamics of the family.

While you'll experience unparalleled joy, you'll also face times of stress, tension, and frank disagreement about a range of topics. Can your marriage withstand the stress? How will a baby change things for you? Discuss these important topics first.

- *Do you share common practical philosophies?* I'm not talking about Kant versus Nietzsche. I'm talking more about cloth versus disposable:

"I never thought that we'd be fighting about issues like whether to let our nine-month-old cry it out, or putting him in daycare versus me staying at home. It's made for a very tense marriage."

The two of you will undoubtedly have some differences of opinion about such issues as child-rearing principles, discipline, and schooling. There are some fundamental things you should agree on—moral issues, values, the importance of the family, and so on. There's nothing worse than the clash of philosophies, especially when the two of you are worn out from a hard day of work, either at home with the baby or outside at your job. While it's impossible to resolve certain issues before they come up, it's vital that the two of you try to anticipate differences and acknowledge their potential to disrupt your joy.

- *Have you considered time-management issues?* Are you ready to make sacrifices? How are you going to work full time, go back to school to get that master's degree in Eastern European Aviary Studies, play softball with the guys, shoot hoops, see your girlfriends, bathe regularly, get your nails done, and have time to play with your baby? These are good questions. If you're the sort of person who has a hard time managing your time, don't worry. A lot of us go on to have great experiences with our kids. However, if you don't think you'll be able to give up your time in the service of raising a healthy child or help your spouse, you need to reconsider.

> Rent and watch every movie you've ever wanted to see before the baby is born.

- *Are there religious or cultural differences?* If so, can you be sure that their impact on your relationship and baby will be positive? Don't forget, most families want very much to be involved in your lives—especially now that you're considering a baby. If there are significant cultural or religious differences, family pressures, disagreements, and other unpleasantness are that much more likely to occur.

- *Can you make decisions together?* If you're both used to making important decisions without consulting one another, you'll probably have a tough time raising a child. There are numerous advantages to making decisions together. If you decide together, you'll rarely have to worry alone—and parents of newborns do a lot of worrying. Making decisions together will also bring the two of you closer:

"I couldn't have done it without my husband."

Working together will also strengthen your resolve and heighten your ability to survive the first few months of your baby's life—a time that offers tremendous joys but also exhaustion and hard work. Being involved with each other will also provide your baby with a more loving and nurturing environment. If you're not able to work as a team—making decisions together, sticking together during trying times, and working together for your baby's future—you should rethink your decision to have a baby now. Work on solidifying your alliance with your partner first.

- *Do you feel settled in your marriage?* Are you certain marriage is for you? As with any other meaningful endeavor designed to last a lifetime, marriage takes time, patience, and perseverance. It may be that you are not quite ready:

"Have a baby now? Gosh, I'm still getting used to my new last name. I really need more time."

There's absolutely nothing wrong with waiting. It's not selfish or unreasonable:

"There's still a lot of stuff my wife and I want to do together before we have a baby. You know, get to know each other better, travel, get settled into the routine of being with someone."

- *Can you share responsibility?* Will you be able to forfeit some control in order to include your spouse in child-rearing? Your baby will benefit greatly from observing your healthy interactions with each other. She'll also benefit from being cared for by both parents—each with his or her own particular style. If you're the kind of person who doesn't like to relinquish control, you should discuss the issue with your spouse.

- *Can you accept responsibility?* Nobody likes being woken up in the small hours of the night. It will happen. Will you be able to share the exhaustion with your spouse? What will it be like if your spouse can't, for some reason, take care of the baby on a particular day? Could you fill in?

- *What about work?* Have you decided who gets to stay home and who goes to work? Will the two of you be able to compromise and work together to come to an equitable resolution? Will you use daycare? Can you be an involved parent and still be a valuable employee or boss?

- *Can you put on hold things that are important to you?* If you are accustomed to certain activities or hobbies, would you be willing to forego them to be there for your baby and spouse?

You can resolve most all of these issues—if not now, then later. Use the time-tested combination of talk, patience, compromise, and humor, and you'll undoubtedly be better off. Remember, if your marriage is on firm ground, you'll have plenty of time to work through the issues of child-rearing.

Your Life Together

The thought of having a baby elicits a lot of different feelings: from a proud sense of maturity to paralyzing dread. Most of the time, though, the issues boil down to timing. It may be that having a baby may not be the best idea for you right now. As the first year winds down, and you begin to consider expanding your family, keep in mind that having a child is a team effort. It's wonderful, meaningful, and fun. While it will ultimately bring the two of you closer together, without teamwork an impulsive decision to have a baby could threaten the structural integrity of your marriage. Make sure your decision is an informed one. Take your time, learn more about yourselves, and enjoy the process.

· *12* ·

Happy Anniversary!

SUCCESSFULLY REACHING YOUR
FIRST YEAR OF MARRIAGE

12

Congratulations! You've both made it. While it's certainly not a race, our hope is that you've both reached the first-year finish line together, holding hands, glancing back over your shoulder to see from where you came but also with an eye on the horizon before you. Who knew the year could fly by so quickly? Whether your year has been challenging or wonderful in nearly every way . . .

"It was like a dream—I wouldn't trade it for anything."

. . . your first married year together symbolized commitment, love, and mutuality. It formed the basis on which the two of you can continue to build, plan for the future, and start your family. If you've had an overall positive experience, you'll want to continue the trend—working together to refine what you've started:

"Looking back, dating and engagement was wonderful. But all along
I never really felt settled or completely content. It was a restless sort of
feeling, like a circle that wasn't closed. Being married very definitely
completes the circle. We've spent the year really just getting to know one
another in ways that weren't possible before. Every aspect of our lives

together has improved—our romance is stronger than ever, we've estab-
lished new friendships, gotten great jobs, and we are saving for a house.
It's been terrific."

Whether the two of you are completely happy together, somewhere in the middle, or struggling with important issues, it's a sure bet
that marriage has changed your lives.

What's New with the Two of You?

As you try to put the year in perspective, try not to worry about competing thoughts. You'll probably have quite a few. In light of the new
and interesting experiences you've had, how could you not? You made
the decision to get married, did it, dealt with your families, discussed
money issues, thought about various legal matters, worked, loved,
played, had a fight or two, said some things you wish you hadn't, made
up, dealt with mixed feelings, developed a social life, reviewed the year,
and may now be thinking about expanding your family. That's a lot of
material to be covered in one year! Of course, no one expects you to
have dealt with all the issues. Remember, marriage is a nonstop, evolu-
tionary process—always changing and renewing itself. Ask questions
and listen to each other for the answers.

YOU MAY BE FEELING . . .

Proud and Confident There are so many reasons to feel this way.
Many married couples may feel proud of their accomplishments together and are confident in their ability to weather any potential
storms. Some couples enjoy being seen out and about, holding hands,
defying the unhappy marriage odds. Or, if you're the sort of person
who had doubts about your ability to love, be loved, or stay true to one
person, take time to delight in your resolve, strength, and success:

"What an ego booster this whole thing has been. I mean, to think that there was someone out there whom I could love and be loved by—it's just fantastic!"

Content   Couples often feel fulfillment—spiritual, social, romantic, and otherwise. Marriage seems to be everything, or nearly everything, they thought it would be.

In Love   What a wonderful concept:

"I feel like I'm more in love with my husband now, a year after our wedding, than I was on our wedding day."

Nostalgic   Many happily married couples are nostalgic for their dating and courting days and talk about that time fondly:

"We decided to go out one day and visit all the places we used to go when we were dating—the restaurants, parks, and so on. It was so wonderful. It brought us closer together."

Reminiscing is a great way to visit the past and everything it signified, and to reaffirm the reasons you're together.

Settled   Your single friends may sometimes refer to you as "the old married couple." Feeling settled can, under most circumstances, be a really nice sensation. For example, being settled is a great thing if the road to marriage or the first year was bumpy and unsettled.

Like a Husband or Wife   Along with all the fun, marriage also encompasses broad responsibility and commitment to a continuing process. While you became a husband or a wife right after you said "I do," sometimes it really doesn't sink in until much later:

"It finally dawned on me, about six months after the wedding: 'Hey, I'm married to someone. I feel grown-up.'"

Ambivalent Mixed feelings come in all different shapes and sizes. Exploring your feelings is part of the human experience. There will be times when you're absolutely sure you've made the right decision and other times when you'll be uncertain. Remember, marriage, like anything else designed to last forever, has to be a fluid, not a fixed, experience.

Confused With so many important things happening during your first year together, it's not uncommon to feel periodically perplexed or bewildered. However, if you feel unhappy and worry about the health of your marriage, your confusion may mean something entirely different:

"It's taken me a year to realize that I'm not entirely happy with this arrangement. I feel confused about it. Should I go on trying to love her? Should I chalk it up to a bad choice? Will it pass? Is it me?"

It often takes a year, or longer, to decide if a bad thing will grow worse or if it can get better:

"By the end of the first year it was obvious that we weren't on the same wavelength. I don't even think we were on the same planet anymore. We went to a counselor who recommended that we consider temporary separation. It wasn't until we were physically separated that I realized how much I loved her. We will make this thing work. We have to."

Depressed or Anxious If things haven't gone right, you could experience feelings of despair, anguish, and depression. Depending on what the two of you decide to do, you'll need to work through the feelings and continue on with your lives—together or apart.

Being There for Each Other

So where are the two of you in the scope of things? How far have you come together? What's left to do? Don't forget that the first year of your marriage has been an incredibly concentrated year. You've probably tried hard to start new traditions, work together as a team, talk, spend time together, and attend to all the details of your lives—money, work, love, and so on. You've gotten pretty good at learning to juggle your new responsibilities and have had to take some well-deserved breaks in between to care for yourself. Given all this, where *should* the two of you be?

Where You Should Be: A One-Year Checklist

Try to keep in mind that these are merely suggestions. As you grow together, you'll both develop your own styles of getting things done. But it's a good idea to check up on each one of these important "spokes" of your marriage. Make sure the structure is sound. If one area is weak, do what you need to do to fix it. Don't wait!

- *Engagement and wedding:* Do you ever stop to consider how far the two of you have come together? Take some time every now and then to review the events surrounding your meeting, dating, engagement, and wedding. Keep your lives in perspective. When you're dealing with tough issues that seem to be dividing you, try to remember these early days. Try to identify the happiness and pleasure that brought you together in the first place. Take an active interest in each other's feelings and anxieties. Laugh together about the funny times and console each other during hard times.
- *Family:* If family issues have been tough to deal with, how have you handled the difficulties? Have you and your husband

talked? Do you approach family problems as a team? Do you feel estranged from either of your families? What are the main issues? Have you been able to forge a positive relationship with your families? Have you started to establish traditions that can be used to include them in your lives? What else can the two of you do to improve your family relationships? By making the most of your families and their love, the two of you can grow closer together.

- *Money:* Take your financial pulse. Is it strong? Weak? Irregular? Do you meet periodically to discuss important money matters? Have you started to save or at least plan out the sorts of things you want in your future? What are your short-term and long-term plans? Do you have emergency money saved? Have money issues gotten in the way of a smooth transition from engagement to marriage? How do you solve money conflicts? Have the two of you updated your financial plan to suit your latest needs?

- *Legal matters:* Don't underestimate the importance of drafting a will and securing disability, health, and life insurance. Do these things now to avoid having to play catch-up after tragedy strikes. If you have a child, these matters are even more crucial. Have you consulted with an attorney? Don't leave your futures up to fate. Act now.

- *Fighting:* What was your last fight about? Can't remember? Well, during the next one, remember that you forgot what your last one was all about. Are you employing patience, compromise, and communication to resolve your problems? Your first fight will not be your last. You want the intensity of your disagreements to mellow with time. Learn to put off more difficult or controversial issues until you've built a foundation for resolving them.

- *Romance:* Is the flame still alive and well? Do you both still enjoy each other's company? If not, why? Do you go out to-

gether? Have you discussed how much your lives have changed
for the better with each other? What can the two of you do to
improve your lives and become even closer?

- *Social lives:* Are you taking care of each other by caring for
yourselves? Have you started to develop some lasting relationships with other couples? What are you doing to stay in shape?
Can you find the time to be together but to also maintain your
sense of individuality?

- *Crumbling marriage:* If things have been tense between the two
of you, have you attended to the main issues or do you hope
the problems just vanish on their own? What seems to be driving you apart? Do you treat each other with respect or have
you become distant? What have you noticed about your relationship that seems different, in a bad way, from your dating
period? What's changed? Are you seeking professional help?

- *Parenthood:* Have you weighed the tremendous benefits
against the awesome responsibility of having children?
What's in it for both of you? What kind of parents will you
be? Do you share similar values? Do you have the time to be
an active, involved parent? Are you thinking about children
for the right reasons?

It Just Keeps Getting Better

It was only a year ago that you each proclaimed your love for one another in front of friends and family. While a lot has undoubtedly
changed, the hope is that the essence of what drew you together remains unchanged. If you've taken some time during the first year to
talk and reflect upon your experiences together—both good and bad—
you're already ahead of the game. As you stand at the threshold of
greater experiences, don't forget that your continuing journey is a trip
built for two. Following are a few tips to help you stay on course.

Tips for Your Anniversary— and Beyond

- *Cherish your time together:* You never know what might happen next.
- *Smile and laugh together as frequently as possible:* Your marriage will endure and you'll live longer.
- *Treat each other with respect, even during those rare occasions when you can't stand to look at each other.*
- *Get in the habit of expressing your feelings—both positive and negative—verbally:* If you're talking, you're not acting out.
- *Respect each other's wishes for periodic time alone.*
- *Tape record or videotape some of your early experiences—shopping, traveling together, or just talking:* Watch or listen to the tapes the next time you have a major blowout.
- *Learn to listen to each other carefully:* When you listen, make your partner feel as if he or she is the only one in the world at that moment.
- *Try not to worry too much about making ordinary mistakes in your relationship:* Unless the mistake is a painful, destructive one, the relationship will survive.
- *Work through your differences using patience, compromise, communication, and humor.*
- *To gain perspective and share great memories, look through your wedding and photo albums together:* Review your book of "firsts" together.
- *Every once in a while, take a symbolic step outside yourselves and watch your marriage from a distance:* Would you want to be in a relationship like that? If not, it's time to work through the problems.
- *Speak to each other with respect:* Don't let degrading profanity contaminate your relationship.
- *Never, ever worry by yourself:* Seek refuge in each other.

- *Remember the old adage "Never go to bed angry":* At the very least, agree to discuss your problems in the morning after you're more rested.
- *Don't be afraid to heap praise on each other when praise is due.*
- *Celebrate your anniversary surrounded by friends and family, or just by being together:* Congratulate each other. It is truly a monumental accomplishment.

Your Life Together

As you make your way through the challenges and pleasures of the years to come, try to always remember why you're together. Admire, encourage, and love each other, as you did on your wedding day. Do your best to make each day better than the one before—through teamwork, love, and respect. If you work together, you'll beat the odds and you can look forward to a life of fulfillment, fun, personal growth, and enduring love. You'll be saying, "I do" to each other—every day—forever:

> *"I'll never forget it. It was sometime during the middle of our first year of marriage. I stood at the dishwasher, overloading it, while my wife was busy burning the macaroni and cheese. We both looked at each other, realizing the absurdity of the situation. We started to talk about where we each had come from, how we found each other, and where we wanted to go. The food continued to burn, the dishwasher door got stuck beyond repair. We laughed. We realized that, for better or worse, we had to cling together, loving, learning, and growing—chuckling about the good times, preparing ourselves for the worst of times. Through sickness and in health, burned food and broken dishwashers, we made our commitment to grow old together, relishing the thought of making all sorts of interesting, great mistakes together. What a team. Nothing could be better."*

Index

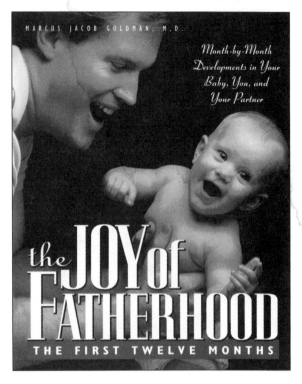